FRANCIS FRITH'S

A Taste of
SCOTLAND

REGIONAL RECIPES FROM SCOTLAND

Illustrated with historical photographs from
The Francis Frith Collection

FRANCIS FRITH'S

A Taste of
SCOTLAND

Ayr, High Street 1900 46002

Compiled by Julia Skinner

First published in the United Kingdom by The Francis Frith Collection in 2011.

Paperback Edition ISBN 978-1-84546–368–7

British Library Cataloguing in Publication Data

A Taste of Scotland
Julia Skinner

The Francis Frith Collection®
6 Oakley Business Park, Wylye Road,
Dinton, Wiltshire SP3 5EU
Tel: +44 (0) 1722 716 376
Email: info@francisfrith.co.uk
www.francisfrith.com

Printed and bound in England on material sourced from responsibly managed forests.

Front Cover: Edinburgh, Princes Street, West End 1897 39113t

The colour-tinting in this image is for illustrative purposes only, and is not intended to be historically accurate.

Every attempt has been made to contact copyright holders of illustrative material. We will be happy to give full acknowledgement in future editions for any items not credited. Any information should be directed to The Francis Frith Collection.

As with any historical database, the Francis Frith archive is constantly being corrected and improved, and the publishers would welcome information on omissions or inaccuracies.

CONTENTS

INTRODUCTION

—·—

Some hae meat that canna eat
And some wad eat that want it:
But we hae meat, and we can eat,
And sae the Lord be thankit.

Travel around Scotland through the pages of this book and discover a selection of the delicious traditional food of the area, as well as some of the stories and fascinating facts behind the recipes. Your journey will be given added savour by the historical images taken by photographers from The Francis Frith Collection, showing the people and places of this beautiful country in the past.

Regional traditional dishes were developed from the local produce that was available to thrifty housewives who had to feed large, hungry families on a limited budget. Many of the old recipes also reflect the limited cookery techniques that were available in the past, as well as the skills of the cooks who were able to provide cheap and tasty meals with only a fire, a skillet and a cauldron to cook with, often producing the historical version of 'boil in the bag' meals.

This book is not intended to provide a comprehensive collection of the local recipes of the country, and some recipes are modern interpretations using some of the fine local produce that Scotland is famous for, but we hope that the food described within these pages will provide you with a true taste of Scotland.

Grace be here, and grace be there,
And grace be round the table;
Let ilka ane take up their spoon
And eat as muckle's they're able.

Stirling, The Bruce Statue 1899 44681

SOUPS

— . —

RECIPE

— . —

Barley Kail Soup

Barley is commonly used in Scottish traditional cookery, and this old Scottish cottage recipe is filling and economical. Traditionally the stock would have been made with mutton bones and a few scraps of meat, so if you have a bone from a roast lamb joint, put that in for extra flavour as well as any leftover pieces of meat, cut into small pieces.

> 50g/2oz pearl barley
> 1.2 litres/2 pints good stock
> 450g/1 lb kale or spring greens, washed and cut into shreds,
>   with coarsest stalks removed
> 3 leeks, washed, trimmed and cut into thin slices
> Salt and pepper

Put the barley and the stock (plus the lamb bone and meat scraps, if using) into a large saucepan, bring it to the boil then reduce the heat, cover the pan and simmer for about 45 minutes, or until the barley is tender, carefully skimming off any scum which rises to the surface. Add the shredded kale or spring greens and the washed and sliced leeks to the pan. Season to taste, and simmer until the vegetables are tender.

— . —

A Shetland Knitter c1890 A001086

Mingulay, Bagpiper Calum Johnstone 1959 M249002

RECIPE

— . —

Scots Broth

This filling soup, also known as Scotch Broth, or Barley Broth, would originally have been made with mutton, but nowadays is more commonly made with lamb.

This broth won the approval of the notoriously hard-to-please Dr Samuel Johnson when he toured Scotland with James Boswell in 1773. 'At dinner, Dr Johnson ate several plate-fuls of Scotch broth, with barley and peas in it, and seemed very fond of the dish. I said, 'You never ate it before?'. Johnson: 'No sir; but I don't care how soon I eat it again.' ('Journal of a Tour to the Hebrides', 1786, James Boswell)

> 1kg/2 lbs lean neck of lamb, cut into small chunks
> 1.75 litres/3 pints water
> 1 large onion
> 50g/2oz pearl barley
> 75g/3oz dried peas (soaked in water overnight) or fresh peas
> 1 bouquet garni
> 1 large carrot, chopped
> 1 turnip, chopped
> 3 leeks, trimmed, thoroughly washed and chopped
> Half a small white cabbage, shredded
> Salt and pepper

Put the lamb and water into a large saucepan, bring to the boil and carefully skim off any scum which rises to the surface. Add the onion, pearl barley, peas and bouquet garni. Partly cover the saucepan, reduce the heat and simmer gently for 1 hour.

Add the remaining vegetables, and season to taste. Bring back to the boil, then cover again and simmer for further 30-40 minutes, until the vegetables are tender.

Skim off any fat from the top of the soup, remove the bouquet garni and serve piping hot.

— . —

Glencoe, The Scene of the Massacre 1890 G81001

RECIPE

—·—

Cock-a-Leekie Soup

This famous Scottish dish is more of a stew than a soup. It is a very old recipe, and was recorded in 1598 when Fynes Morrison described a dish he had eaten whilst dining at a knight's house in Scotland: '··· but the upper messe, insteede of Porredge, had a Pullet with some prunes in the broth'. There is a story that the soup originated in the days when cockfighting was a popular sport, and the losing cock was eaten after the contest, thrown into a stock pot with some leeks. The addition of prunes for extra flavour was a later refinement, although some cooks nowadays often omit these, or remove them before serving. The prunes can either be used whole, or stoned and roughly chopped if preferred.

> 1 small chicken about 1.2kg (2 lbs 10oz)
> 6-8 thick leeks, trimmed, washed and roughly chopped,
>   keeping the green and white parts separate
> 6 black peppercorns
> 2 bay leaves
> 12 prunes, soaked in cold water for several hours
> 2 tablespoonfuls finely chopped fresh parsley
> Salt to taste

Put the chicken in a large saucepan. Add the green parts of the leeks, the peppercorns, bay leaves and just enough water to cover the chicken. Bring slowly to the boil then reduce the heat, cover the pan with a tight-fitting lid and simmer for 20-25 minutes. Remove from the heat, keep the pan covered and leave for about 1 hour, until the chicken is cooked and tender. Remove the chicken from the pan carefully and place in a sieve over a bowl. When cool enough to handle, remove and shred the flesh, discarding the skin and bones.

Meanwhile, remove and discard the green leeks, peppercorns and bay leaves from the pan, and add the white leeks. Simmer gently until the leeks are tender, and add salt to taste. Return the chicken flesh to the pan together with the prunes, reheat gently and serve in a warm bowl, sprinkled with parsley.

—·—

RECIPE

— · —

Cullen Skink

Cullen Skink is a famous traditional Scottish recipe from the Moray Firth for a rich and creamy smoked haddock soup. 'Skink' comes from a Gaelic word which originally meant 'essence', but now describes a stew-like soup, whilst 'cullen' was the name for the 'seatown' (port or harbour) district of a town.

700g/1½ lbs smoked haddock (the un-dyed variety is best to use)
600ml/1 pint milk
600ml/1 pint water
2 onions, peeled – chop one onion and leave the other whole
1 blade of mace
50g/2oz butter
3 medium-sized potatoes, peeled and chopped into chunks
Salt and freshly ground black pepper
1 tablespoonful finely chopped fresh parsley
4 tablespoonfuls single cream
Chopped fresh parsley or chives, to garnish

Place the fish in a large saucepan, cover with the milk and water and add the whole onion and the mace. Bring slowly to the boil over a gentle heat, then reduce the heat and simmer very gently for 5 minutes. Remove the pan from the heat and leave to stand for 10 minutes. Strain off the cooking liquid and reserve.

In another saucepan, melt the butter, add the chopped onion and chopped potatoes and cook over a gentle heat for about 10 minutes, stirring occasionally, until the onion has started to soften. Pour the reserved, strained cooking liquid into the pan and simmer gently, until the potato pieces are soft. Remove from the heat and allow to cool slightly, then pass through a sieve or liquidize in a blender. Rinse out the saucepan, then return the liquidized soup to it.

Flake the cooked fish, being careful to remove all the bones and the skin, and stir the fish flesh into the soup. Add salt and freshly ground black pepper to taste, stir in the cream and reheat gently before serving. Serve with a garnish of finely chopped fresh parsley or chives.

— · —

Greenock, Custom House Quay 1897 39814

Glen Turret, Grouse Shooting 1900 45957x

RECITE

—·—

Game Soup

1 onion
1 carrot
1 stick of celery
75g/3oz butter
1.2 litres/2 pints game stock, made from the carcasses of
    2 game birds (such as pheasant, grouse, partridge)
Any meat picked from the carcasses, finely chopped
1 bay leaf
Salt and pepper
25g/1oz plain flour
2 teaspoonfuls redcurrant jelly
2 tablespoonfuls sherry or red wine
2 teaspoonfuls lemon juice

Peel and chop the onion, scrub and chop the carrot, and wash and slice the celery. Melt 50g (2oz) of the butter in a large pan, and sauté the vegetables for 2-3 minutes, turning them over from time to time, until they are lightly browned. Add the stock, bay leaf, and salt and pepper to taste. Bring to the boil then reduce the heat, simmer gently for 1 hour, then strain and discard the vegetables and bay leaf. Melt the remaining butter in another pan, stir in the flour to make a roux and cook gently for 2-3 minutes, stirring. Gradually add the strained liquid to the roux, a little at a time, stirring continually so that no lumps are formed. Bring to the boil, then reduce the heat, add the finely chopped meat and simmer for 5 minutes. Just before serving, add the lemon juice, redcurrant jelly and sherry or wine. Reheat until the jelly has dissolved, then serve immediately.

—·—

RECIPE

— . —

Tattie Soup

This traditional soup based on 'tatties' (potatoes) is a filling and tasty way of using up old vegetables. The addition of bacon is optional, but does improve the flavour significantly. In past times, in the spring a handful of finely chopped young nettle sprigs would have been added to the soup a few minutes before serving, to add extra nutritional value, but modern cooks will probably prefer to use parsley instead.

        450g/1 lb old potatoes
        2 large old carrots
        2 onions
        4 rashers of streaky bacon with the rinds cut off (optional)
        1.7 litres/3 pints of good stock
        Salt and freshly ground black pepper, to taste
        A handful of finely chopped fresh parsley (or nettle tops)

Peel the potatoes and cut them into very thin slices. Peel the onions and trim and scrape the carrots, and either chop them very fine, or coarsely grate them. Cut the de-rinded bacon into small pieces.

Bring the stock to the boil in a large saucepan, then add the prepared vegetables and the bacon. Reduce to simmer, cover the pan and leave to cook gently for 1½ -2 hours, until the vegetables have cooked right down and the soup has become thick. (If a smoother texture is preferred, remove the soup from the heat at this stage and allow to cool a little, then pass through a sieve or liquidize in a blender and return to the pan and heat through again.) Season to taste, and add the chopped parsley (or nettles, to be really authentic!) just before serving.

— . —

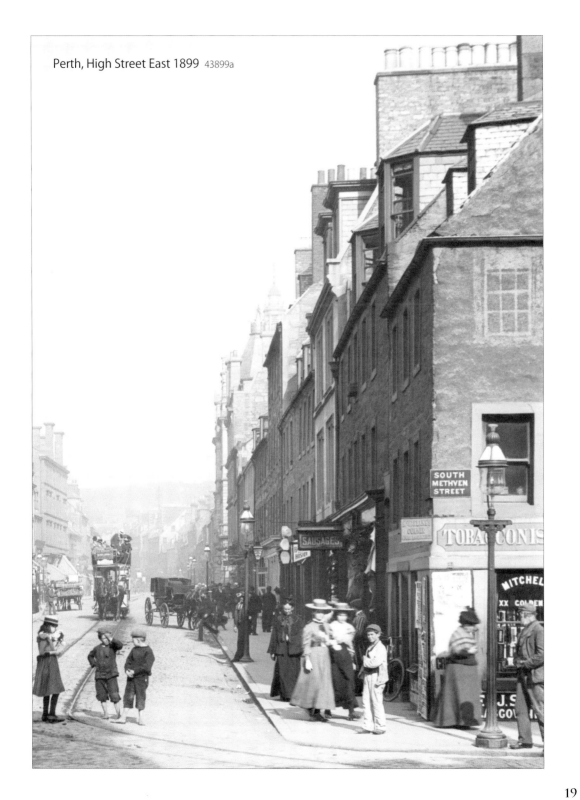

Perth, High Street East 1899 43899a

FISH

Fraserburgh, The Herring Fleet F63002

Herring were an important catch for Scottish fishermen in the 19th and early 20th centuries. Herring, known to fishermen as the 'silver darlings', are very nutritious and used to be a staple part of most people's diet. Hunting the herring was a perilous business, but when the drift nets were hauled in, near bursting with fish, it was a time for rejoicing, as the Scottish poet Hugh Macdiarmid described:

O it's ain o' the bonniest
Sichts in the warld
To watch the herrin' come
Walkin' on board
In the wee sma' 'oors o'
A simmer's mornin'
As if o' their ain accord.

Chasing the Silver Darlings

Herring shoals were pursued in deep seas far from the harbour, and the journey home was too long for the fish to be sold and eaten fresh; some method of preserving them was essential, and the herring were usually salted and dried. The number of boats drifting for herring increased, and gutting and curing houses sprang up in the ports of north-east England and Scotland. The industry was seasonal, which led to migrations of labour from port to port; the fishing harbours would be thronged with men and women working hard to meet the sailing schedules, ensuring that catches were not forfeited and vital income lost. Gutting and packing the fish was done by women. This was a skilled job, and a good herring woman could gut 40 fish a minute. As the women were on piece-rate it was essential to keep their fingers nimble, which they did by continuously knitting in their free time.

In Scotland, drifting for herring was particularly hazardous, because of the shallow-decked boats favoured by the Scots fishermen. In the photograph opposite of Fraserburgh, a major port on the north-east coast, the harbour is crowded with open boats from ports around the region, with men arranging the tackle ready for sailing, and folding and stowing the huge drift nets with their floats. The vessel in the foreground is from Nairn, further west along the Moray Firth. Though she is broad in the beam, her decking is shallow to allow nets to be pulled on board easily, and would offer scant protection in the violent storms of the North Sea. The Scottish writer Sir Walter Scott famously commented on the fishing industry: 'It's nae fish ye're buying, it's men's lives'. In 1848 there was a tragic disaster when a hundred Scottish fishermen were lost in a ferocious south-easterly gale. Despite an enquiry and a strong appeal for a change to safer decked luggers, the Scottish fishermen, and their own Fisheries Board, remained unconvinced by the arguments, and it was not until 1872 that the first decked boat was built.

RECIPE

— . —

Herring with Mustard Sauce

In this recipe the herring are filled with a savoury stuffing and served with mustard sauce for a tasty lunch or supper. Mustard sauce is a traditional accompaniment to herring in many parts of Britain, and is also served with boiled or poached cod in Scotland. Serves 4.

4 large herring
3 heaped tablespoonfuls fresh white breadcrumbs
1 heaped teaspoonful finely chopped parsley
A squeeze of lemon juice
Grated rind of half a lemon
Salt and black pepper
Oil for frying
25g/1oz butter
Lemon wedges and fresh parsley sprigs for garnish

Pre-heat the oven to 200°C/400°F/Gas Mark 6.

Remove the heads from the herring, clean, gut and bone them, then wash the fish and pat them thoroughly dry. Put the breadcrumbs, parsley, lemon juice and lemon rind in a basin, and season lightly with salt and freshly ground black pepper. Melt the butter and stir it into the breadcrumbs to bind the mixture, which should now be moist, but crumbly.

Stuff the fish with the breadcrumb mixture, and if necessary secure them with wooden cocktail sticks. Slash the skins crossways two or three times on each side; brush the herring with oil and wrap each fish separately in foil. Put the herring in a well-buttered deep ovenproof dish; cover with lightly buttered greaseproof paper and bake in the centre of the pre-heated oven at for 35-40 minutes. Just before the fish are cooked, make the mustard sauce as directed on page 23. Transfer the baked herring to a hot serving dish and garnish with wedges of lemon and sprigs of parsley. Serve the mustard sauce separately.

— . —

Mustard Sauce

40g/1½ oz butter
25g/1oz plain flour
450ml/ ¾ pint milk
Salt and black pepper
1 level tablespoonful dry mustard powder
1 tablespoonful wine vinegar
1 level teaspoonful caster sugar

Melt 25g/1oz of the butter in a pan; stir in the flour and cook for 1 minute. Gradually stir in the milk, beating well until the sauce is quite smooth. Bring to the boil and simmer for 2-3 minutes; season with salt and pepper. Blend the mustard powder with the vinegar and stir into the sauce, and add the sugar. Check seasoning and stir in the remaining butter.

Aberdeen, The Fish Market c1900 A90316

RECIPE

— . —

Herring in Oatmeal

There would be as much activity on shore as on the boats themselves in Scotland's fishing towns and villages. The Scottish fishwives and their children were kept busy collecting mussels for bait, mending nets, and knitting jerseys. Often the fishwives had to do the job of selling the fish as well, and when landings were late owing to bad weather, they were obliged to haul the laden baskets of fish several miles to the markets to negotiate with wholesalers.

This is a popular and traditional way of eating herring in Scotland. Serves 2-4 depending on appetite.

> 4 herring
> 2 tablespoonfuls oatmeal
> Half a teaspoonful salt
> Pepper
> Fat for frying

Scale and clean the herring and wash and dry them well. Mix the oatmeal with the salt and pepper and use this to coat the fish on both sides, pressing the oatmeal well into them. Fry in hot fat for 5 minutes each side. The herring can also be grilled if preferred, prepared in the same way, but frying gives them more flavour.

— . —

Coldingham, A Scottish Fish Wife c1932 C358024x

'Caller Herrin, Caller Ou'

These cottages at Newhaven, Fife, are an example of the type of fishermen's dwellings that could be found in past times around Scotland's harbours, usually single-storey terraces with slate or stone roofing. These cottages at Newhaven had a characteristic outside stair to the first-floor door, and below were storerooms for nets and sails. At Newhaven the fishermen's wives were noted for the way they dressed, which was said to reflect the community's Dutch and Scandinavian origins. They were also famous for their street cries when selling fish at the markets in Edinburgh: 'Caller Herrin' (fresh herring) and 'Caller Ou' (fresh oysters).

Newhaven, Fishermen's Cottages 1897 39137

RECIPE

—·—

Haddock and Prawns in Cheese Sauce

If fresh haddock is hard to find, other white fish such as coley, hake or whiting can be used instead.

4 fresh haddock fillets
12 peeled prawns
50g/2oz plain flour
50g/2oz butter
300ml/ ½ pint milk
50g/2oz Cheddar cheese, grated
1 small onion, peeled and very finely chopped
Salt and cayenne pepper
90ml/3fl oz double cream

Pre-heat the oven to 200°C/400°F/Gas Mark 6. Coat each haddock fillet lightly with seasoned flour. Use half the butter to grease a shallow ovenproof dish and then arrange the fish fillets in a single layer in this. Melt the remaining butter in a small pan and stir in the flour. Cook gently for 2-3 minutes, stirring occasionally. Gradually blend in the milk, a little at a time and stirring continually so that no lumps are formed, then add the grated cheese and very finely chopped onion. Increase the heat and cook, stirring, until the sauce has thickened. Roughly chop the prawns and stir into the sauce. Season the sauce to taste with salt and cayenne pepper, and stir in the cream. Pour the sauce over the fish fillets in the dish. Bake in the centre of the pre-heated oven for 30 minutes. If the top has not browned by the end of the cooking time, place the dish under a pre-heated grill for a few minutes before serving.

—·—

RECIPE

—·—

Smoked Haddock Tart

Scottish fish, whether caught from the lochs, the sea or the fast-running streams and rivers, is superb. For centuries the Scots have been masters of the art of smoking fish, and the smoked salmon, haddock, kippers and bloaters produced in Scotland are unsurpassed. Smoking fish is one of the oldest ways of preserving food. In ancient and medieval times the smokehouses used oak and other woods to create dark-smoked haddock such as the famous Arbroath smokies that are still produced in Scotland (they actually originated in Auchmithie rather than Arbroath, but the latter village became the major producer). In the mid 19th century the milder, lighter smoked haddock (the Finnan Haddock – known as 'haddie') became popular. It came originally from the village of Findon, just south of Aberdeen. Haddie is a lightly salted, delicately smoked whole fish, originally dry-salted and smoked over peat for some 8 hours. Try to buy naturally smoked fish if possible, without the bright yellow dye.

225g/8oz shortcrust pastry
A little beaten egg to seal the pastry
2 tablespoonfuls chopped fresh parsley
450g/1 lb smoked haddock fillets
150ml/ ¼ pint milk
A few black peppercorns
3 bay leaves
A few sprigs of fresh parsley
50g/2oz butter
2 onions, finely chopped
3 tablespoonfuls skinned cucumber, chopped into small cubes
1 tablespoonful chopped fresh chives
3 tablespoonfuls plain flour
175ml/6fl oz single cream
Salt and freshly ground black pepper
115g/4oz Cheddar cheese, grated

—·—

—·—

Pre-heat the oven to 200ºC/400ºF/Gas Mark 6, and place a baking tray in the oven to heat up. Roll the pastry out on a floured surface sprinkled with 1 tablespoonful of the finely chopped parsley, and use it to line a large, shallow, greased tart or flan tin or dish. Put a piece of greaseproof paper with some baking beans on the pastry base, place the tin or dish on the pre-heated baking tray in the oven and bake blind for 15 minutes (this helps the pastry base to cook through). Remove from the oven and take out the greaseproof paper and baking beans. Prick the pastry base all over with a fork, brush the pastry case all over with beaten egg to seal it, and return to the oven for a further 5-10 minutes, until the pastry has turned a light golden brown.

Place the haddock fillets in a wide-bottomed frying pan with a lid. Cover the fish with the milk and add the peppercorns, bay leaves and sprigs of parsley. Bring gently to the boil with the lid on, then turn the heat off and leave the pan for 5-10 minutes. Take the haddock fillets out of the pan using a slotted spoon (reserve the cooking liquid), then break up the fish into small flakes, being sure to remove and discard any bones, and set the fish aside. Melt the butter in a separate pan, add the onions and fry for about 10 minutes or until they are quite soft, stirring occasionally. Add the diced cucumber, the remaining chopped parsley and the chopped chives, stir in the flour and cook gently for 2 minutes. Strain the reserved liquid from cooking the fish. Gradually stir the strained fish liquid and cream into the onion mixture, a little at a time, stirring continually so that no lumps are formed, and continue to cook, stirring, over a low heat until the sauce thickens. Add salt and pepper to taste, then add the grated cheese, reserving a handful for the top. Add the flaked fish to the sauce and then transfer it all into the pre-baked pastry case. Sprinkle the tart with the reserved cheese. Bake in a pre-heated oven at 190°C/375°F/Gas Mark 5 for 30 minutes, or until the filling is risen and brown, and firm to the touch.

—·—

RECIPE

— · —

Finnan Pancakes

1 egg, beaten
175g/6oz plain flour
900ml/1½ pints milk
75g/3oz butter
225g/8oz smoked Finnan haddock
Salt and pepper
2 eggs, hard-boiled and chopped into pieces
1 dessertspoonful finely chopped fresh parsley

Place 115g (4oz) of the flour in a bowl and stir in the beaten egg. Gradually blend in 300ml (½ pint) of the milk to form a smooth batter. Take 25g (1oz) of the butter to cook the pancakes. Heat a little of the butter in a frying pan. When the butter is hot, pour in sufficient batter to thinly coat the bottom of the pan. Brown on one side, then turn the pancake and brown the other side. Remove the pancake from the pan and keep to one side. Use the batter to make more pancakes – this amount should make about 8.

Cook the smoked haddock very gently in 300ml (½ pint) of the milk until it is tender. Lift out the cooked fish with a slotted spoon and drain, reserving the cooking liquid. Break up the fish into small flakes, being sure to remove and discard any bones.

Pre-heat the oven to 190°C/375°F/Gas Mark 5. Make up the liquor that the fish was cooked in to 600ml (1 pint) with the remaining cold milk. Melt the remaining 50g (2oz) of butter in a saucepan, then stir in the remaining flour and cook gently for 2-3 minutes, stirring occasionally. Gradually add the liquid, a little at a time and stirring continually so that no lumps are formed. Bring to the boil, stirring, until the mixture thickens, then reduce the heat and cook gently for a few minutes. Mix half the sauce with the flaked fish, and season to taste. Divide the filling between the pancakes, then roll up the pancakes and arrange them in a wide, greased ovenproof dish. Stir the chopped hard-boiled eggs into the remaining sauce, season to taste, then spread the sauce over the stuffed pancakes. Bake in the pre-heated oven for 15-20 minutes. Serve sprinkled with chopped fresh parsley.

— · —

Dunoon, West Bay 1897 39829

Arran, The Castle and Loch Ranza c1890 A93001

RECITE

— . —

Scottish Salmon with Dill Butter Sauce

Scotland's salmon and trout rivers are world-famous. The Tay, the Dee, the Spey, the Tweed and many others are all well-stocked with salmon, sea-trout and brown trout. However, in Scotland salmon fishing is not just a sport for anglers but an important commercial livelihood for fishermen on both the east and west coasts. Scottish salmon, whether fresh or smoked, is unsurpassed. Serves 4.

> 4 salmon steaks
> 50g/2oz butter, softened to room temperature
> Finely grated rind of half a lemon
> 1 tablespoonful lemon juice
> 1 tablespoonful finely chopped fresh dill
> 2 lemon slices, cut into halves
> 4 sprigs of fresh dill
> Salt and freshly ground black pepper, to taste

Place the butter, lemon rind, lemon juice, chopped dill and salt and pepper in a bowl, and mix it well together with a fork, to make the dill butter. Spoon the butter mixture on to a piece of greaseproof paper and roll it up to form a sausage shape. Twist the ends together, wrap in cling film and place in the freezer or ice box of the fridge for 20 minutes, until it is firm.

Pre-heat the oven to 190°C/375°F/Gas Mark 5. Cut out four pieces of foil each big enough to encase a salmon steak, grease them lightly and place a salmon steak in the centre of each piece of foil. Remove the butter from the freezer, unwrap and slice it into 8 rounds. Place two rounds of the dill butter on top of each salmon steak with one of the lemon pieces between them, and place a sprig of dill on top. Bring up the edges of the foil to encase each piece of salmon in a foil parcel and crinkle the edges to seal firmly. Place the salmon parcels on a baking sheet and cook in the pre-heated oven for 20-25 minutes. Remove from the oven, undo the foil and slide the salmon steaks with their topping on to warmed serving plates, pour the juices from the parcel on to each salmon steak and serve.

— . —

'Glasgow Salmon'

The incorporation of salmon in the Glasgow arms reflects the enormous importance to the city of the River Clyde, for the bounty of its fish. So plentiful was salmon in the 17th century that servants in the city stipulated that they should not be forced to eat it more than twice a week! No salmon could have survived in the industrially-polluted river of the 19th and early 20th centuries, but in the post-industrial city of the 21st century salmon – and many other species of fish – are once more in the Clyde.

Glasgow, The Broomielaw 1897 39799

RECIPE

— · —

Tweed Kettle

The Tweed is one of the great salmon rivers of Scotland. This method of preparing salmon comes from Edinburgh, where it was a 19th-century speciality. Tweed Kettle, also known as Salmon Hash, is traditionally served with 'bashed neeps' (see page 70) or 'tatties' (mashed potatoes).

900g/2 lbs fresh salmon, from the tail end if possible, gutted and cleaned
150ml/ ¼ pint dry white wine
115g/4oz mushrooms, finely sliced
25g/1oz butter
2 shallots, very finely chopped, or 2 tablespoonfuls of
    finely chopped fresh chives
150ml/ ¼ pint water that the fish is cooked in
A pinch of ground mace
2 tablespoonfuls finely chopped fresh parsley
Salt and freshly ground black pepper

Place the fish in a fish kettle or large saucepan and just cover it with water. Slowly bring the water to the boil, then reduce the heat and simmer very gently for 5 minutes. Remove the salmon from the pan, and remove the skin and any bones. Return the skin and bones to the cooking liquid, bring it back to the boil and simmer for 15 minutes, then strain the liquor, measure out 150ml (¼ pint) and put this into a clean pan.

Cut the cooked fish into cubes about 5cm (2 inches) square, and place this into the pan with the cooking liquid, together with the white wine, chopped shallots or chives, mace and seasoning to taste. Cover the pan and simmer gently for 20 minutes. Melt the butter in a frying pan, add the sliced mushrooms and sauté until they are beginning to soften. Add the drained mushrooms to the salmon, cook for a further 5 minutes and then serve, garnished with chopped fresh parsley.

— · —

RECIPE

—·—

Scottish Smoked Salmon, Cucumber and Herb Tart

A little beaten egg for the pastry base
1 large cucumber, skinned and chopped into small chunks
Salt and freshly ground black pepper
225g/8oz smoked salmon, broken into good-sized pieces
225g/8oz cream cheese, or soft cheese such as Philadelphia
2 eggs, plus 1 extra egg yolk
150ml/ ¼ pint double cream
2 tablespoonfuls finely chopped fresh parsley
2 tablespoonfuls finely chopped fresh chives
2 tablespoonfuls finely chopped fresh dill
Finely grated zest of 1 lemon
Juice of 1 lemon

Pre-heat the oven to 200ºC/400ºF/Gas Mark 6, and place a baking tray in the oven to heat up. Roll out the pastry on a lightly floured surface, and use it to line a large, shallow, greased tart or flan tin or dish. Place a piece of greaseproof paper with some baking beans on the pastry base, place the tin or dish on the pre-heated baking tray in the oven and bake blind for 15 minutes. Remove from the oven and take out the greaseproof paper and baking beans. Prick the pastry base all over with a fork, brush the pastry case all over with beaten egg to seal it, and return to the oven for a further 5-10 minutes, until the pastry has turned a light golden brown.

Put the chopped pieces of cucumber in a colander and sprinkle lightly with salt. Cover the cucumber with a small plate and put a heavy object or two on top of the plate – this acts as a 'press' to force out some of the superfluous liquid from the cucumber. Place the colander in a bowl or in the sink and leave for 30 minutes, by which time some of the superfluous water will have drained away. Rinse the cucumber, then drain and dry in kitchen paper.

Arrange the cucumber pieces, together with the smoked salmon, in the pre-baked pastry case. Put the cream or soft cheese, eggs, egg yolk, cream, herbs and lemon zest and juice into a bowl with salt and pepper to taste and beat or whisk together until well mixed. Spoon the cheese mixture over the salmon and cucumber in the pastry case. Bake in the oven at 200°C/400°F/Gas Mark 6 for 30 minutes, or until the tart is cooked but not dry, and the filling is firm to the touch. This can be eaten warm or cold.

—·—

MEAT, POULTRY AND GAME

Haggis and Robert Burns

Fair fa' your honest sonsie face
Great chieftain o' the puddin' race!
(From 'To a Haggis', Robert Burns)

Robert (Rabbie) Burns, thought by many to have been Scotland's greatest poet, was born in a simple cottage at Alloway on 25th January 1759. The cottage, a 'but and ben', or two-room clay cottage, was built by the poet's father, a gardener from Kincardineshire, and later became an inn. In 1881 the cottage was purchased by the trustees of the Burns Monument and opened as a museum. The pleasant village of Alloway is now the centre of pilgrimage for lovers of Burns's poetry. Robert Burns died in Dumfries in 1796 at the early age of thirty-seven.

The life and works of Robert Burns are celebrated each year in Scotland on Burns' Night, 25th January, with a special Burns' Night Supper. Much merrymaking takes place, special toasts are drunk and traditional dishes are eaten – especially Scotland's most famous dish, haggis. Haggis is rather like a large, oval-shaped sausage, made from a sheep's stomach stuffed with oatmeal and the minced or chopped parts of an animal which might otherwise be discarded, such as the heart, lungs and liver (the finest haggis uses liver from a deer, rather than a sheep). Haggis is traditionally served with Bashed Neeps – see page 70. At Burns' Night celebrations the haggis is brought in to the accompaniment of a piper, and placed ceremoniously before the chief guest. 'To a Haggis' by Robert Burns is then recited, and the haggis is toasted with drams of whisky before being eaten.

Queen Victoria was served haggis whilst staying at Blair Castle in 1844, and recorded her thoughts in 'Leaves of a Highland Journal': 'There were several Scottish dishes, two soups and the celebrated haggis, which I tried and really liked very much.'

Portrait of Robert Burns (1759-1796)
39858a

RECITE

— . —

Scots Collops

'Collop' is an old word for a slice of meat. A dish of collops of venison, beef or lamb is traditionally served in Scotland on Burns' Night, 25th January. This recipe uses collops of fine Scottish beef.

> 4 onions, peeled and sliced
> 115g/4oz mushrooms, finely chopped
> 50g/2oz butter
> 1 tablespoonful oil, for frying
> 4 thin slices of Scottish rump steak
>   – about 1cm (½ inch) thick
> Salt and pepper

Heat the butter and oil together in a large frying pan and fry the onions until they are well-browned and cooked through. Remove them to a hot dish and keep warm.

Increase the heat and fry the steak slices in the remaining fat in the pan, allowing 2-3 minutes on each side, then remove the steaks to the dish with the onions, stir them around a little with the onions and season to taste with salt and pepper. Keep hot.

Add the mushrooms to the frying pan, season to taste and cook gently until their juices are running a little. Tip out the mushrooms and the cooking juices on top of the steaks, and serve immediately.

— . —

RECIPE

—·—

Aberdeen Angus Steaks with Whisky Sauce

This is a luxury recipe for a special occasion, using the finest Scottish beef steaks with an indulgent whisky sauce. This quantity serves 4 – if you are only cooking for two, halve the quantities for the sauce.

115g/4oz butter
1 onion, peeled and finely chopped
4 Aberdeen Angus fillet steaks, about 175g (6oz) each in weight
Salt and freshly ground black pepper
4 tablespoonfuls of whisky
115g/4oz mushrooms, thinly sliced
1 teaspoonful coarse-grain mustard
300ml/ ½ pint beef stock
150ml/ ¼ pint cream

Melt the butter in a frying pan and gently sauté the finely chopped onion until it is soft and transparent, then increase the heat and add the steaks. Cook the steaks for 3-5 minutes on each side depending on their thickness and individual preference. Remove the steaks to a hot dish and keep warm whilst the sauce is prepared.

Drain off the excess fat from the pan and add the whisky. Use a wooden spoon to stir up the residue from the bottom of the pan and mix in all the juices. Add the stock, mustard and sliced mushrooms. Increase the heat to boil the sauce and reduce it down to a thick syrup. Reduce the heat, add the cream and heat through gently. Season the sauce to taste, then pour it over the steaks and serve immediately.

—·—

Aberdeen, Union Street
c1900 A90309

RECIPE

Aberdeen Roll

225g/8oz streaky bacon rashers, rinds removed
225g/8oz minced beef
1 large onion, peeled and very finely chopped
75g/3oz rolled oats
1 tablespoonful Worcestershire sauce
1 teaspoonful made mustard
Salt and pepper
1 egg, beaten
Approximately 150ml/ ¼ pint stock

Pre-heat the oven to 180°C/350°F/Gas Mark 4 and grease a loaf tin.

Chop the de-rinded bacon rashers into very small pieces. Mix the bacon and finely chopped onion with the minced beef. Add the oats, Worcestershire sauce, mustard, salt and pepper and the beaten egg and mix it all well together, adding a little stock if the mixture is dry.

Press the mixture firmly into the greased loaf tin and cover with foil. Stand the tin in a small, deep-sided roasting tin and pour in enough boiling water to come halfway up the sides of the loaf tin. Bake in the pre-heated oven for 2 hours.

When cooked, turn out of the tin and serve cut into slices. This can be either eaten hot, served with a tomato sauce, or cold.

Aberdeen, The Market Cross 1892 A90302

Elgin, Little Cross 1890 E56004

RECIPE

— · —

Sausage and Kidney Hotpot

4 sheeps' kidneys

4 large sausages

115g/4oz bacon rashers with the rinds removed

3 small onions, peeled and chopped

115g/4oz mushrooms, sliced

225g/8oz carrots, cut into short, very thin strips

25g/1oz butter

15g/ ½ oz plain flour

300ml/ ½ pint stock

1 teaspoonful tomato purée

1 tablespoonful sherry

Salt and pepper

Remove the skins from the kidneys, cut them into 4 pieces and cut out the core. Take the skins off the sausages and form the meat from each sausage into 2 or 3 small balls. Cut the de-rinded bacon into pieces. Melt the butter in a pan and fry the bacon until the fat runs. Add the chopped kidneys and sausagemeat balls and fry them quickly until they are lightly browned, then remove the meat from the pan and put to one side. Add the chopped onions and sliced mushrooms to the pan and cook gently for about 5 minutes, stirring occasionally.

Stir the flour into the pan and let it cook for 1 minute, then stir in the tomato purée. Gradually add the stock, a little at a time, stirring continually so that no lumps are formed, then add the sherry. Increase the heat and bring to simmering point, stirring continually as the sauce thickens. Season to taste with salt and pepper. Add the carrot strips and the cooked bacon, kidney and sausagemeat balls. Cover the pan with its lid, reduce the heat and simmer gently for half an hour.

— · —

Abbotsford, From the Tweed 1890 A92001

In 1811 the popular author Sir Walter Scott purchased the Cartley Hole estate in Teviotdale, on the banks of the Tweed, and changed its name to Abbotsford. Abbotsford House was designed in the baronial style by Scott himself and built between 1817 and 1824, complete with a steam central heating system. It includes an armoury where Scott's collection of weapons is displayed.

RECIPE

—·—

Teviotdale Pie

This dish originates from the border region of Teviotdale, and is the kind of filling suet pie which was made in the past to stretch a small amount of meat to feed a hungry family.

> 450g/1 lb lean minced beef
> 1 onion, peeled and chopped
> 300ml/ ½ pint beef stock
> 1 teaspoonful Worcestershire sauce
> 225g/8oz self-raising flour
> 25g/1oz cornflour
> 75g/3oz shredded suet
> Salt and pepper to taste
> 300ml/ ½ pint milk

Pre-heat the oven to 180°C/350°F/Gas Mark 4.

Place the minced beef in a large saucepan and cook it over a medium heat in its own fat until it starts to brown. Add the onion and cook for a further 5 minutes, until the onion is softened. Add the stock and Worcestershire sauce, and simmer for 20 minutes.

Put the flour, cornflour, suet, salt and pepper into a bowl, then gradually stir in the milk, a little at a time so that no lumps are formed, to form a thick batter.

Put the meat and its gravy into a 1.2 litre (2 pint) pie dish, then cover with the batter mixture. Bake in the pre-heated oven for 30-35 minutes until the topping is risen and browned.

—·—

Edinburgh, The Scott Monument 1897
39112

The Scott Monument in Edinburgh
commemorates the 19th-century
author Sir Walter Scott. Inside the
monument are 287 steps to the top.

RECITE

— . —

Chicken in the Heather

Use Scottish heather honey for this roast chicken dish if possible, for a true flavour of Scotland, but otherwise any clear honey can be used.

> One roasting chicken, about 1.5kg/3½ lbs in weight
> 90ml/3 fl oz cooking oil
> 115g/4fl oz clear heather honey
> Salt and freshly ground black pepper
> 75g/3oz made mustard
> Half a teaspoonful curry powder
> One clove of garlic, finely chopped

Pre-heat the oven to 190°C/375°F/Gas Mark 4.

Place the chicken in a large ovenproof casserole dish. Mix all the other ingredients together and pour the mixture over the chicken. Cover the dish with its lid and cook in the pre-heated oven for 1 hour.

Baste the chicken thoroughly with the juices and sauce in the dish, then remove the lid and return to the oven to cook, uncovered, for a further 30-40 minutes – this will then brown the chicken.

Serve with boiled or mashed potatoes and fresh seasonal vegetables.

— . —

RECIPE

— · —

Stoved Chicken

'Stoved' in the name of this dish derives from the French word 'étouffer' which means to steam by cooking in a covered pot, a relic of the French influence on Scottish cooking that resulted from the 'Auld Alliance' between Scotland and France in the 17th century.

> 1kg/2 lbs potatoes, peeled and cut into thin slices
> 2 large onions, peeled and cut into thin slices
> 1 tablespoonful chopped thyme, fresh if possible
> 25g/1oz butter
> 1 tablespoonful cooking oil
> 2 large slices of bacon, de-rinded and chopped into small pieces
> 8 chicken drumsticks or thighs, or a combination of both
>   (or 4 large chicken joints, each cut in half)
> 600ml/1 pint chicken stock
> Salt and freshly ground black pepper to taste

Pre-heat the oven to 150°C/300°F/Gas Mark 2. Place a layer of sliced potatoes on the bottom of a large ovenproof casserole. Cover with half the onion slices, and sprinkle with half the chopped thyme, and season to taste.

Heat the butter and oil together in a large frying pan, then brown the chicken pieces on all sides, together with the bacon pieces. Transfer the chicken and bacon to the casserole, reserving the fat in the frying pan. Sprinkle the chicken with the rest of the chopped thyme and season again lightly, then cover the chicken with the remaining sliced onions and then the potato slices, overlapping them neatly on top, and season again to taste. Pour the chicken stock into the casserole, then brush the reserved fat from the frying pan over the potato slices.

Cover the casserole with a tightly fitting lid, and cook in the pre-heated oven for about 2-2½ hours, until the chicken is really tender. When cooked, remove the lid from the casserole and place the dish under a hot, pre-heated grill for a few minutes, to brown and crisp the potato slices before serving immediately.

— · —

RECIPE

—. —

Dunelm of Chicken

A dunelm is a Scottish version of a hash that can be made with either cold leftover chicken or veal, usually including cream and mushrooms.

> 225g/8oz cold chicken
> 115g/4oz small mushrooms
> 50g/2oz butter
> 150ml/ ¼ pint chicken stock
> Salt and freshly ground black pepper
> Juice of half a lemon
> 4-5 sprigs of fresh tarragon, finely chopped
> 3 tablespoonfuls double cream
> 2 slices of white bread, with their crusts removed
> Oil for frying the bread

Cut the chicken into small, thin pieces, about 2cm (1 inch) square. Slice the mushrooms thinly. Melt the butter in a large saucepan and cook the mushrooms gently until they are softened and limp. Add the chicken stock, salt and pepper, lemon juice and chopped tarragon and bring it to the boil. Boil hard until the liquid has reduced by half, then add the cream and boil for 4 minutes. Add the chicken to the sauce and reduce the heat. Leave to cook gently until the chicken is heated through, but do not let it boil.

Cut each bread slice into four triangles. Heat some oil in a frying pan and fry the bread on both sides until it is golden and crisp. Serve the dunelm of chicken on warmed plates accompanied by the fried bread triangles (or 'sippets').

—.—

Strathpeffer, Wringing the Washing c1890 S421003

Grouse

In Britain, the main shooting season officially begins with grouse on 'the glorious twelfth' of August. The grouse season then lasts from 12th August to 10th December. The popularity of grouse reached its height during the Victorian era, when Queen Victoria's annual move to Balmoral with the rest of the royal family in late summer made shooting in the Highlands a fashionable sport amongst the aristocracy. Four varieties of grouse exist in Scotland, the Capercaillie, the Black Grouse, the White Grouse (Ptarmigan) and the Red Grouse. The strong, dark meat of red grouse is considered by some to be the finest of all game birds. Young birds are best cooked wrapped in bacon rashers and roasted, and in the Highlands are sometimes stuffed with wild raspberries, rowanberries or cranberries, mixed with butter. Older birds which have escaped the guns for some years are not usually tender enough for plain roasting, but can be made into a tasty casserole such as the recipe on the opposite page, which is flavoured with herbs and brandy.

Balmoral Castle, From the South West c1890 B268002

RECILPE

~·~

Grouse with Brandy and Cream Sauce

4 mature grouse
10 button onions (or shallots)
1 stick of celery
225g/8oz mushrooms
115g/4oz butter
About 3 level dessertspoonfuls of plain flour
600ml/1 pint stock
Fresh thyme, marjoram and rosemary, finely chopped
Salt and black pepper
4 tablespoonfuls of double cream
2 tablespoonfuls of brandy
Juice of half a lemon
4 slices of white bread, with the crusts removed
1 dessertspoonful of finely chopped fresh parsley

Peel the onions but leave them whole. Scrub the celery and trim the mushrooms, and chop both roughly. Melt half the butter in a flameproof casserole dish. Put the whole onions and the trussed grouse into the pan, and cook in the butter until the grouse are browned on all sides. Take out the grouse and onions and put to one side.

Put the celery and mushrooms into the casserole and fry in the remaining butter until soft. Stir in as much flour as is needed to absorb all the fat, and cook gently for a few minutes, stirring occasionally. Gradually blend in the stock, stirring all the time. Increase the heat and continue to stir until the sauce has thickened, then reduce the heat and simmer. Add the herbs and season to taste with salt and pepper. Return the grouse and the onions to the casserole dish, cover with its lid and leave to simmer over a low heat on top of the cooker for about 1½ hours, or until the grouse are tender. Just before serving, mix the cream and brandy together, blend in 3 tablespoonfuls of sauce from the casserole and then stir it all into the casserole dish. Add the lemon juice to sharpen the taste, then adjust the seasoning if necessary.

Melt the remaining butter in a frying pan and fry the bread slices on both sides until they are crisp and golden. Drain on kitchen paper, then arrange the slices on a hot serving dish. Place one grouse on each piece of fried bread, pour over a little of the sauce, and sprinkle them with chopped fresh parsley. Serve the rest of the sauce separately in a sauce boat. Serves 4.

~·~

RECIPES

—·—

Venison Casserole

1kg/2 lbs 4oz venison braising steak, cut into cubes
2 tablespoonfuls plain flour, seasoned
50g/2oz butter
2 tablespoonfuls oil
2 onions, peeled and thinly sliced
1 clove of garlic, peeled and finely chopped
600ml/1 pint stock
150ml/ ¼ pint red wine
1 tablespoonful tomato purée
225g/8oz carrots
115g/4oz mushrooms
2 dessertspoonfuls redcurrant jelly
Salt and freshly ground black pepper

Pre-heat the oven to 180°C/350°F/Gas Mark 4. Toss the cubes of venison in the seasoned flour so that all sides are covered. Melt half the butter and oil together in a flameproof casserole that has a tight-fitting lid. Fry the venison in batches, a few cubes at a time, until all sides are browned. Put the browned meat to one side and keep warm. Melt the remaining butter and oil in the casserole, add the sliced onions and cook gently for about 10 minutes, until they are soft and transparent, then add the finely chopped garlic. Stir in the remaining seasoned flour and cook for 1-2 minutes, then add the tomato purée, and then the stock and the red wine, a little at a time, stirring continually. Increase the heat and bring the sauce to the boil, constantly stirring as the sauce thickens. Season to taste with salt and pepper, then add the sliced carrots and mushrooms and the browned venison pieces. Put the lid on the casserole and cook in the pre-heated oven for about 1½ - 2 hours. Stir the redcurrant jelly into the casserole 10 minutes before serving. This casserole is even better if it is made the day before needed, and reheated in the oven before serving.

—·—

Venison Pot Roast

Until the 1700s much of Scotland's population ate wild venison, but after the landowners claimed the Highlands for sheep runs, the poor could usually only obtain this meat by poaching. Nowadays the development of farmed venison has helped revive its popularity, and it is much more readily available to everyone. Venison is a rich and well-flavoured meat, low in cholesterol and high in iron. It can sometimes be dry, but a good way of cooking it is in a pot roast, stew or casserole, to make sure it is tender and juicy.

1.75kg/4-4½ lbs boned joint of venison
5 tablespoonfuls of oil
4 cloves
8 black peppercorns, lightly crushed
12 juniper berries, lightly crushed
250ml/8fl oz red wine
115g/4oz smoked streaky bacon, chopped into small pieces
2 onions, finely chopped
2 carrots, chopped
150g/5oz mushrooms, sliced
1 tablespoonful plain flour
250ml/8fl oz stock
2 tablespoonfuls redcurrant jelly
Salt and pepper

Marinade the venison the day before needed: place the joint in a bowl, add half the oil, the spices and the wine, cover and leave in a cool place for 24 hours, turning the meat occasionally so that all sides absorb the flavour.

Pre-heat the oven to 160°C/325°F/Gas Mark 3. Remove the venison from the marinade and pat it dry with kitchen paper. Reserve the marinade to use later. Heat the remaining oil in a large shallow saucepan, and brown the venison evenly on all sides. Transfer the meat to a large casserole dish. Add the bacon, onions, carrots and mushrooms to the saucepan the venison was browned in, and cook for about 5 minutes. Stir in the flour and cook gently for 2 minutes, stirring all the time, then remove the pan from the heat and gradually stir in the marinade liquid, stock, redcurrant jelly and seasoning to taste. Return the pan to the heat and bring to the boil, stirring continually, then reduce the heat and simmer for 3 minutes. Pour the sauce into the casserole dish with the venison, cover the dish with its lid and cook in the oven for about 3 hours, until the meat is really tender. Turn the meat occasionally in the dish whilst it is cooking. Serve the venison cut into slices, with the sauce and vegetables spooned over.

The Forth Bridge 1897 39145

CHEESE, EGG AND VEGETABLE DISHES

Eriskay, Western Isles 1963 E188009

RECITE

—·—

Crowdie Eggs

Crowdie is a Scottish fresh cheese which was traditionally made by crofters. The name comes from the Scots word 'cruds', meaning 'curds'. This modernized version of Crowdie makes a herb-flavoured savoury spread, ideal as a sandwich filling or spread onto oatcakes.

 1.2 litres/2 pints milk
 Juice of half a lemon
 Salt and freshly ground black pepper
 3 hard-boiled eggs, peeled and finely chopped
 Grated zest of 1 lemon
 1 tablespoonful finely chopped fresh chives
 1 tablespoonful finely chopped chervil
 2 spring onions, trimmed and finely chopped
 1 tablespoonful mayonnaise

Put the milk in a bowl or jug and add the lemon juice, then leave to stand for 20-30 minutes, to sour. Transfer the milk to a saucepan and place over a very low heat, until it is just warm but not simmering, until the liquid whey has separated from the solid curds. Remove from the heat and allow to cool, then drain off the whey. Line a colander with a clean tea towel or a piece of muslin and stand it in a bowl, then pour in the curds. Leave until most of the remaining whey has drained through, then gather up the corners of the cloth and squeeze the curds until the last of the liquid has drained out. Tip out the curds into a bowl, add a pinch of salt and beat well with a wooden spoon until the curds are smooth. Put the chopped hard-boiled eggs into another bowl and mix with the lemon zest, chives and chervil, mayonnaise and freshly ground black pepper. Fold the egg mixture into the curds until well mixed. Spoon the mixture into a serving dish (or small individual dishes if preferred), and sprinkle the top with the chopped spring onions. Chill for at least 30 minutes before serving.

—·—

RECIPE

— . —

Sliced Potatoes and Onions Baked in Milk

Potatoes arrived in Britain from the New World in the 16th century, and soon become an everyday food – until then, parsnips formed a major source of carbohydrate in the British diet. Potatoes were most important in the food history of Scotland, since they opened up formerly marginal lands for food production and supplemented grain harvests – a contribution of critical importance in areas such as Scotland, where the climate made cereal production so problematical. For cooking purposes, potatoes can be divided into floury or waxy types. Floury potatoes, good for baking, mashing and making chips, are more popular, particularly in Scotland. Farm carts selling 'mealy tatties' – floury potatoes – were a familiar sight in 19th-century Scottish streets.

This makes a good accompaniment to game and meat dishes.

> 75g/3oz butter
> 6 medium to large potatoes, peeled
> 3 onions, peeled
> 600ml/1 pint milk
> Salt and freshly ground black pepper

Pre-heat the oven to 170°C/325°F/Gas Mark 3.

Use some of the butter to liberally grease a shallow ovenproof dish. Slice the potatoes and onions as thinly and evenly as possible. Arrange alternate layers of potato and onion in the dish, dotting each layer with small knobs of butter, and seasoning each layer as you go. Pour on enough milk to come just below the top of the potatoes, and bake in the pre-heated oven for 1½ hours.

— . —

Linlithgow, At the Cross Well 1897 39157x

RECIPE

— · —

Potato, Onion and Bacon Hotpot

This makes a tasty, filling and cheap supper dish. Either bacon rashers, scraps of cooked bacon leftover from a boiled joint or bacon off-cuts from a butcher can be used. A couple of tablespoonfuls of grated cheese can also be added to the sauce, if preferred. Do not be too heavy-handed with the salt, as the bacon will add a certain amount of saltiness to the dish anyway. Often known as 'Stovies' in Scotland, this can also be made with leftover cooked meat such as beef and lamb, cut into pieces.

> 4 large potatoes, peeled and cut into thin slices
> 4 large onions, peeled and cut into very thin slices
> 175-225g/6-8oz bacon
> 600ml/1 pint milk
> 50g/2oz plain flour
> 50g/2oz butter or margarine
> Salt and pepper

Pre-heat the oven to 200°C/400°F/Gas Mark 6.

If using bacon rashers, remove the rind, and cut the bacon into small pieces. Grease a casserole with a tight-fitting lid. Fill it with alternating layers of sliced onions, sliced potatoes and bacon pieces, ending with a layer of potatoes.

Melt the butter or margarine in a saucepan, stir in the flour and cook gently for 2 minutes. Add the milk, a little at a time, stirring continually so that no lumps are formed. Bring to the boil, stirring constantly until the mixture thickens. (Add the grated cheese now, if using, and stir until it has melted.) Reduce the heat, season to taste, and simmer the sauce for 5 minutes. Pour the white sauce over the bacon and vegetables in the casserole, then give the casserole a good shake to distribute the sauce evenly.

Cover the casserole with its lid and bake in the pre-heated oven for 1 hour, then remove the casserole lid, reduce the oven temperature to 150°C/325°F/Gas Mark 4 and bake for a further 1 hour.

— · —

Gourock, Kempock Street 1900   45978

Ben Nevis, From Corpach 1890 B267001

Ben Nevis, known to both locals and visitors as 'The Ben', is the highest mountain in the British Isles. Popular with climbers, Ben Nevis is located at the western end of the Grampian mountains, near the Highland town of Fort William. The name of the mountain is an Anglicised version of the Scottish Gaelic 'Beinn Nibheis'. 'Beinn' means 'mountain', but there are several possible meanings of 'Nibheis' – it is most commonly translated as 'malicious', but it may derive from 'nèamh-bhathais', meaning 'heavens' (from 'nèamh') and 'top of a man's head' (from 'bathais'), giving a more romantic interpretation of 'the mountain with its head in the clouds', or perhaps 'mountain of Heaven'.

RECIPE

— . —

Bashed Neeps

Bashed Neeps is the traditional accompaniment to haggis, but is also good with meat and sausages. This dish is made with 'brassica rapa', otherwise known as 'rutabaga' or 'Swedish turnip', which is called 'swede' in England. This vegetable was introduced into Scotland in the late 18th century by Patrick Miller of Dalswinton, a director of the Bank of Scotland and also Chairman of the Carron Iron Company. One of Carron's customers, King Gustav III of Sweden, sent Mr Miller a bejewelled snuff-box containing rutabaga seeds, knowing that he had a keen interest in all things agricultural. The snuff-box and the accompanying letter are now in the British Museum.

> 450g/1 lb swede (Swedish turnip),
>   peeled and cut into small pieces
> 50g/2oz butter
> Salt and freshly ground black pepper
> A pinch of mace or ground nutmeg (optional)

Cook the swede (Swedish turnip) in boiling water for 25-30 minutes, until it is tender. Drain well. Add the butter, salt and freshly ground black pepper to taste, and mace or nutmeg if used. Mash well until the butter is melted and thoroughly mixed in.

— . —

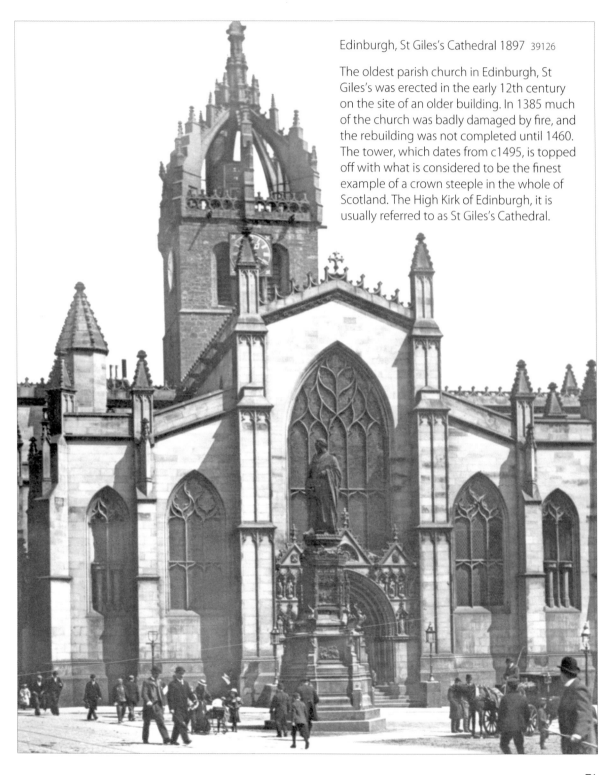

Edinburgh, St Giles's Cathedral 1897 39126

The oldest parish church in Edinburgh, St Giles's was erected in the early 12th century on the site of an older building. In 1385 much of the church was badly damaged by fire, and the rebuilding was not completed until 1460. The tower, which dates from c1495, is topped off with what is considered to be the finest example of a crown steeple in the whole of Scotland. The High Kirk of Edinburgh, it is usually referred to as St Giles's Cathedral.

RECIPE

— · —

Rumbledethumps

This wonderfully-named dish is also known as Kailkenny in some parts of Scotland (when cream is used instead of butter). It can either be eaten as a supper dish or as an accompaniment to roast meat or stews. Some versions omit the cheese topping, and others include mashed carrots and turnips.

> 450g/1 lb potatoes, cut into small cubes
> 450g/1 lb cabbage, chopped into small pieces
> 50g/2oz butter or margarine
> 1 large onion, peeled and finely sliced
> Salt and freshly ground black pepper
> 50g/2oz grated hard cheese of choice

Cook the potatoes in boiling water until they are tender. Drain well, then mash. Boil the cabbage until it is tender. Melt the butter in a large saucepan and fry the onion gently until it is soft. Add the mashed potatoes and cabbage, season to taste and mix well.

Pre-heat the oven to 190°C/375°F/Gas Mark 5.

Turn the mixture into a greased shallow ovenproof dish and cover with the grated cheese. Cook in the pre-heated oven for about 20 minutes, until the top is browned.

— · —

Edinburgh, John Knox's House 1897 39125

PUDDINGS AND DESSERTS

Rothesay, The Pier 1897 39836

Rothesay is in an ideal location in the sheltered 'sweet Rothesay Bay', to quote the popular song. It is the county town on the eastern side of the Island of Bute. The pier has changed little from how it appears in this photograph: in the holiday period it is still as busy as it was a century ago. The main sailing destinations from Rothesay are to Wemyss Bay on the Ayrshire coast and, in the summer season, to the Island of Arran. In this photograph it is 1897, and a golden age for the Clyde excursion steamer industry is dawning, as the ban on landings at some piers on the Sabbath will soon be broken. As one paddler loads, another leaves the pier. The paddler pulling away might be the 'Ivanhoe', shortly after her sale to the Caledonian Steam Packet Co, but before her paddle-boxes were painted white and a bar installed. The ship was always immaculately turned out, and her crew wore naval uniform. In 1894 she spent a couple of months on charter on excursion work along the newly opened Manchester Ship Canal, but returned north in time for the summer season.

RECIPE

— . —

Dunfillan Bramble Pudding

Wild blackberries, or brambles, grow in many parts of Scotland, although they are less common in the Highlands. They are ripe from early August until late September, and have a much better flavour than the commercially grown blackberries available in supermarkets nowadays – and it's much more fun to go out in the countryside foraging for them. This delicious pudding has a layer of blackberries beneath a sponge topping.

For the fruit layer:	For the topping:
450g/1 lb blackberries (brambles)	115g/4oz self-raising flour
115g/4oz caster sugar	50g/2oz butter or margarine,
A very small pinch of salt	softened to room temperature
A pinch of ground cinnamon	50g/2oz caster sugar
(optional)	1 egg
1 tablespoonful water	A pinch of salt
	2 tablespoonfuls milk
	Grated zest of 1 lemon

Pre-heat the oven to 180°C/350°F/Gas Mark 4 and butter an ovenproof pie or pudding dish.

Put the blackberries in a heavy-bottomed pan and add one tablespoonful of water. Cover the pan with its lid and cook over a gentle heat until the juice begins to run from the berries and they are just soft. Spoon the berries and most of the juice into the prepared pie or pudding dish in layers, sprinkling each layer with sugar. Add the salt and cinnamon, if using, to the final layer.

To make the topping, beat the butter or margarine and sugar together until the mixture is light and fluffy. Beat the egg and gradually mix it in, a little at a time, then beat in the flour, salt, milk and lemon zest. Spread the mixture smoothly over the fruit, and bake in the pre-heated oven for 20-30 minutes, until the sponge topping is risen and golden brown, and firm to the touch. Serve with cream or custard.

— . —

RECITE

— · —

Cranachan

This famous recipe is one of Scotland's most delicious desserts, and features the raspberries that Scotland is famous for. The raspberries produced in Scotland are renowned for their flavour, due to their slow ripening in the cool Scottish summers. The main areas of what is regarded by many as Scotland's 'national fruit' are in Tayside, especially the Strathmore valley, but raspberries are also cultivated commercially in Grampian, the Highlands, Arran, the borders and Ayrshire, which is noted for particularly fine fruit. Scotland is also the home of the tayberry, a large conical berry with a bright purple colour and a rich flavour, which was developed at the Scottish Crops Research Institute by crossing a raspberry with a blackberry.

50g/2oz medium oatmeal
4 tablespoonfuls clear runny honey
3 tablespoonfuls whisky
300ml/ ½ pint double cream
350g/12oz raspberries

Toast the oatmeal in a shallow layer on a sheet of foil under the grill for a few minutes, stirring occasionally, until it is evenly browned but not burnt. Leave to cool. Whip the cream in a large bowl until soft peaks form, then use a large metal spoon to gently fold in the oats, honey and whisky until well combined.

Reserve a few raspberries for decoration, then layer the remainder with the oat mixture in four serving dishes. Cover and chill for 2 hours.

About 30 minutes before serving, transfer the glasses to room temperature. Decorate with the reserved raspberries and serve.

— · —

Edinburgh, The Clock, Hope Street
1897 39114

RECIPE

— . —

Fig Dumpling

175g/6oz dried figs, soaked overnight in water
    with a squeeze of lemon juice.
225ml/8fl oz milk
150g/5oz self-raising flour
1 teaspoonful baking powder
175g/6oz sugar
115g/4oz shredded suet
50g/2oz fresh breadcrumbs
1 egg, beaten

Cut the stalks off the figs and place them in a shallow saucepan with the milk, and stew them very gently over a low heat for about 10 minutes. Sift the flour and baking powder into a mixing bowl, then mix in all the other dry ingredients. Make a well in the centre, pour in the stewed figs and the milk and beat well to combine thoroughly. Mix in the beaten egg.

Grease a large, heatproof pudding basin and pour in the mixture. Cover the basin with a lid of greased, pleated greaseproof paper and another lid of foil, and tie down securely. Place the pudding basin in a large saucepan and pour in enough water to come halfway up the sides of the basin. Bring the water to the boil, then cover the pan with its lid and steam the pudding for 2-2½ hours, topping up the pan with more boiling water when necessary – do not let the pan boil dry.

Turn out on to a warm serving dish and serve with custard.

— . —

Inverlochy, The Castle c1890 I30001

Glasgow, George Square 1897 39759

RECIPE

— . —

Cloutie Dumpling

This dish takes its name from the 'clout', or cloth, in which the pudding would have been boiled in the past – sprinkling some flour onto the cloth makes it watertight. The instructions for boiling this in a pudding cloth are given here, and also a modern equivalent, for steaming the pudding in a basin. Cloutie Dumpling is a favourite dish for Christmas time.

225g/8oz plain flour, sifted	115g/4oz stoned dates, finely chopped
115g/4oz oatmeal	1 rounded teaspoonful bicarbonate
200g/7oz caster sugar	of soda
1 teaspoonful ground cinnamon	1 teaspoonful golden syrup
1 teaspoonful mixed spice	2 eggs, beaten
115g/4oz shredded suet	250ml/9fl oz milk
225g/8oz mixed currants and sultanas	A little extra caster sugar, to finish.

Put the flour, oatmeal, sugar, cinnamon, mixed spice, suet, dried fruit and bicarbonate of soda in a bowl. Mix well together, then add the golden syrup, the beaten eggs and as much of the milk as necessary to make a soft but firm batter. Dip a tea towel into a bowl of boiling water, then drain well and lay out flat on a board. Sprinkle the cloth with flour, then a little sugar. Place the dumpling mixture in the middle of the cloth, then tie up the pudding by bringing up the corners of the cloth and securing with string, allowing some room for the dumpling to expand. (Alternatively, use a greased pudding basin, covered with a lid of greased, pleated greaseproof paper, to allow room for expansion, and then another lid of foil, tied down securely with string.) Place a trivet or an upturned saucer in a large saucepan and stand the wrapped pudding (or pudding basin) on top of it. Pour just enough boiling water into the pan to cover the pudding. Cover the pan tightly, bring the water back to the boil then simmer gently for 3-3½ hours. Check the water level from time to time and top up the pan with more boiling water when necessary, so that it does not boil dry. When the cooking time is done, finish the pudding in the oven, as below.

Pre-heat the oven to 180°C/350°F/Gas Mark 4. Remove the pudding carefully from the pan and dip it briefly into a bowl of cold water, to prevent the cloth sticking. Cut the string and remove the cloth, then invert the dumpling onto an ovenproof plate (or turn out from the pudding basin). Bake in the pre-heated oven for 10-15 minutes to finish, or until the skin feels slightly less sticky. Sprinkle with caster sugar and serve at once, with cream or custard.

— . —

Braemar, Clearing Snow from Cairnwell Pass 1879 B266003x

RECIPE

— · —

Edinburgh Fog

This rich and delicious dessert should be served accompanied with fresh fruit such as the raspberries for which Scotland is famous.

> 300ml/ ½ pint cream, double or whipping
> 1 tablespoonful caster sugar
> 1 teaspoonful vanilla sugar
> (caster sugar in which a vanilla pod has been stored)
> 50g/2oz chopped blanched almonds
> 50g/2oz small ratafia biscuits
> A small amount of sherry for sprinkling

Whisk the cream until it is stiff. Use a large metal spoon to fold in the sugar, vanilla sugar and chopped blanched almonds.

Spread out the ratafias on a plate, sprinkle them lightly with the sherry and then stir them very gently into the cream mixture.

Serve the 'fog' in a bowl, with a larger bowl of raspberries set beside it.

— · —

Edinburgh, The Castle from the Grassmarket 1897 39121x

TEATIME AND BAKING

— · —

RECIPE

— · —

Sultana Cake

225g/8oz sultanas

115g/4oz butter or margarine

175g/6oz sugar

2 eggs, beaten

A few drops of almond essence

175g/6oz self-raising flour

A pinch of salt

Cover the sultanas with water in a bowl and soak them overnight. The next day, put the sultanas and water into a saucepan and bring the water to the boil, then strain the sultanas and whilst they are still hot mix them with the butter or margarine. Stir in the sugar, eggs and a few drops of almond essence, then sift in the flour and salt, and mix it all together well.

Pre-heat the oven to 180°C/350°F/Gas Mark 4. Grease a 20cm (8 inch) round cake tin, and line the bottom of the tin with greaseproof paper.

Tip the cake mixture into the prepared tin and smooth the top. Bake in the pre-heated oven for 30 minutes, then lower the oven temperature to 150°C/300°F/Gas Mark 2, and continue to bake until the cake is firm to the touch and a metal skewer inserted into the centre comes out clean.

— · —

RECIPE

— · —

Potato Scones

These scones are very popular in Scotland. They can be eaten either an accompaniment to savoury dishes, such as a bowl of soup, or as a teatime treat, spread with jam.

> 200g/7oz potatoes (use a floury variety), peeled and cut into chunks
> 25g/1oz butter
> 50g/2oz plain flour
> ¼ teaspoonful salt
> ¼ teaspoonful baking powder
> A little cooking oil for brushing the griddle or frying pan

Cook the potatoes in boiling water until tender. Drain thoroughly and return the potatoes to the pan, then add the butter and mash until smooth.

Sift the flour, salt and baking powder into a bowl and add the warm mashed potatoes. Mix it all well together to make a soft dough. With floured hands, shape the dough into two balls, then roll each piece of dough out on a floured board to form two rounds about 5mm (¼ inch) thick. Prick all over the dough with a fork and cut each piece into quarters.

Heat a griddle or heavy-based frying pan to medium-hot, and brush it very lightly with oil. Transfer four quarters of the scone dough to the hot griddle or frying pan and cook them for 3-4 minutes on each side until they are golden brown. Repeat with the remaining quarters. Transfer to a wire rack to cool.

— · —

Glasgow, Sauchiehall Street 1897 39763

Tradition says that Glasgow is where the first tea-room was opened, where women could meet and take refreshment – the coffee-houses which had developed in the 18th and 19th centuries were the haunts of men only. This social development was pioneered by a Miss Kate Cranston, later to be Mrs Cochrane, who in 1884 rented rooms in Aitkin's Hotel in Argyle Street, for her tea-shop. Her business was so successful that she later acquired further premises in Buchanan Street, Ingram Street and 217 Sauchiehall Street – now the Willow Tea Rooms, above Henderson's the Jewellers – in a building designed by Charles Rennie Mackintosh.

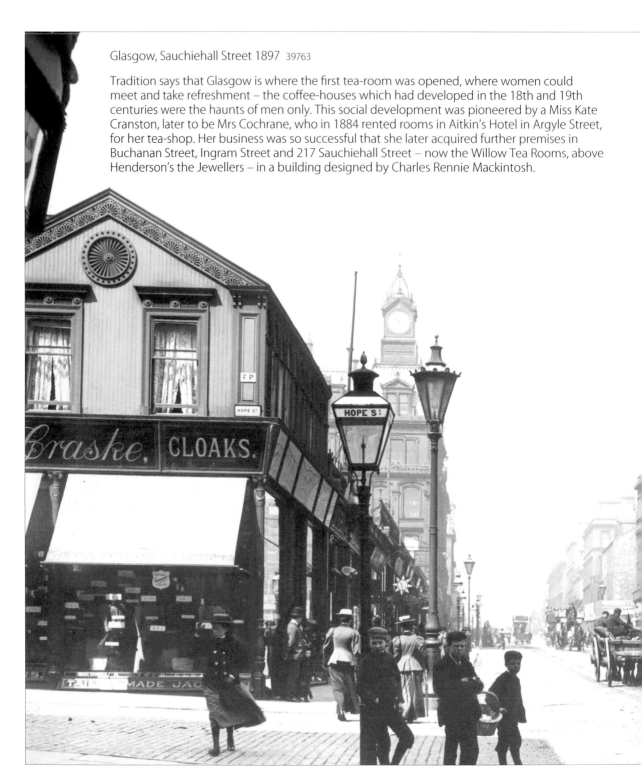

RECIPE

—·—

Buttermilk Scones

What could be nicer at teatime than a freshly cooked scone – something that is now enjoyed all over Britain, but which originated from Scotland's wonderful baking tradition. The name 'scone' comes from the Gaelic word 'sgonn', meaning either 'a lump of dough', or 'a large mouthful', and should be pronounced like 'gone', rather than 'cone'. This recipe calls for buttermilk, which is rather like runny yoghurt. It can be found in most large supermarkets – look for it in the cream section – and makes these scones very light and soft. If buttermilk proves hard to find, use soured milk, either bought or made at home by stirring 1 teaspoonful of lemon juice into 150ml (¼ pint) of milk, then setting it aside for 1 hour to set. Scones are always best eaten on the day they are made, preferably warm from the oven, and spread with butter and jam.

> 225g/8oz plain flour
> 1 level teaspoonful baking powder
> A pinch of salt
> 25g/1oz butter or margarine
> 150ml/ ¼ pint buttermilk
> (or soured milk if buttermilk proves hard to find)
> ¼ teaspoonful bicarbonate of soda

Pre-heat the oven to 220°C/425°F/Gas Mark 7.

Sift together the flour, baking powder and salt. Rub in the butter or margarine until the mixture resembles fine breadcrumbs. Dissolve the bicarbonate of soda in the buttermilk and stir into the dry ingredients, until you have a soft, elastic white dough. Knead lightly until the dough is smooth and the sides of the bowl are clean. Roll out the dough very gently on a lightly floured surface to about 15mm (¾ inch) thick, or press out the dough with your hands. Use a sharp cutter to stamp out the dough sharply into rounds – do not twist the cutter as you press down, as this affects the rising of the scones.

Place the rounds on a greased baking sheet and bake in the pre-heated oven for 10 minutes, then reduce the heat to 200°C/400°F/Gas Mark 6 and cook for a further 5-10 minutes, until the scones are lightly browned.

—·—

RECISE

—. · —

Shortbread

225g/8oz plain flour
115g/4oz caster sugar
115g/4oz semolina or ground rice
225g/8oz butter, cut into small pieces
A little more caster sugar to finish

Pre-heat the oven to 150°C/325°F/Gas Mark 3.

Mix the flour, sugar and semolina or ground rice together in a bowl, then rub in the butter with your fingers until the mixture resembles fine breadcrumbs.

Grease and flour a shallow, round baking tin (18-20cm/7-8 inches in diameter) with butter, or a special shortbread mould if you have one, and press the mixture evenly into it to a thickness of about 2cms (¾ inch). Press around the edge of the dough with your thumb to make a pattern, prick the mixture all over with a fork, and mark it into 6-8 sections.

Alternatively, you can press out the dough on a piece of baking paper until it is a little larger than a 15cm (6 inch) plate, then place the plate on top and cut around it to make a circle of dough. Remove the plate, crimp round the edges of the dough with your finger and thumb, then prick it all over with a fork and mark it into sections, then transfer the dough on the baking paper to a baking sheet.

Bake in the pre-heated oven for about 40 minutes, or until the shortbread is a pale golden colour and just firm to the touch. Leave to cool in the tin, then sprinkle with a little extra caster sugar and cut into sections before serving. Store in an airtight container

—. · —

Glasgow, Buchanan Street 1897 39767

RECIPE

—·—

Black Bun

Black Bun has been popular in Scotland since the 18th century. It was originally made for Twelfth Night, but is now more usually eaten at Christmas and Hogmanay (see opposite page), when it is served to visitors with a glass of whisky. Black Bun is best made 2-3 months before Christmas and stored, wrapped in foil, in an airtight tin, to allow the flavour to mature.

For the pastry:
450g/1 lb plain flour
¼ teaspoonful salt
225g/8oz butter

For the filling:
350g/12oz self-raising flour
1 teaspoonful cinnamon
1 teaspoonful ground ginger
¼ teaspoonful black pepper
¼ teaspoonful ground nutmeg

450g/1 lb seedless raisins
450g/1 lb currants
50g/2oz mixed peel (optional)
50g/2oz glacé cherries
115g/4oz blanched almonds,
    coarsely chopped
115g/4oz chopped walnuts
2 tablespoonfuls whisky
A small amount of milk
2 egg yolks, beaten

Preheat the oven to 180C/350°F/Gas Mark 4. Mix the flour and salt together and rub in the butter until the mixture resembles fine breadcrumbs. Stir in 1 tablespoonful of cold water, and mix well to form a pastry dough. Grease either a loaf tin or a round cake tin. Set aside a piece of pastry for the lid, then roll out the remainder on a lightly floured surface to about 5mm (¼ inch) thick. Line the loaf or cake tin with the pastry, moulding it against the sides and making sure there are no holes.

Mix all the dry ingredients for the filling together and stir well. Add the whisky and stir in, and then enough milk to bring it to a stiff consistency. Fill the tin with the mixture and smooth it off flat at the top. Roll out the pastry lid and lay it on loosely so that the cake mixture can rise a little. Push a long skewer through the lid and filling right to the bottom, in about 8 places. Lightly prick the lid all over with a fork, then brush the lid with the beaten egg yolks. Bake in the pre-heated oven for 2½ - 3 hours until done – test by inserting a skewer into the centre, which should come out clean when the bun is cooked through. Allow the bun to stand in the tin on a wire tray for about 30 minutes before turning out. Serve in slices.

—·—

Hogmanay and First-Footing

A guid New Year to ane an' a' and mony may ye see!

There are various theories about the origin of the word 'Hogmanay', the Scottish name for New Year's Eve on 31st December. One is that is comes from the Norse word 'hoggunott', or 'the night of slaughter', when animals were killed for the midwinter feast of Yule. Another is that it derives from the Flemish phrase 'hoog min dag', or 'great love day', and yet another is that its origin is in the Gaelic words 'oge maidne' for 'new morning', but one of the most widely accepted interpretations is that it comes from the French phrase 'Homme est né', or 'man is born'. Hogmanay is a very important festival in Scotland, even more so than Christmas. There are several Scottish traditions linked with it, such as 'redding', when the house is thoroughly cleaned on 31st December in readiness for the celebrations later that night, and opening the doors and windows of the house, so that as the old year departs it will take its bad luck with it. Offering food such as Black Bun and shortbread to guests who visit also plays an important part in the Hogmanay celebrations. The first person, or 'first-footer', to cross the threshold of a house after midnight on New Year's Eve should be a propitious one, preferably a tall, dark stranger, and it is the custom to make your Hogmanay visits bearing gifts such as salt, bread, whisky or a lump of coal, to ensure good fortune to the household for the coming year – if a visitor arrives empty-handed, ill fortune will follow for the ensuing year. The first-footer is also supposed to enter the house through the front door, and leave through the back. It is traditional to sing 'Auld Lang Syne' (by Robert Burns) immediately after midnight on Hogmanay, and this custom has now become widespread all over the British Isles on New Year's Eve.

Should auld acquaintance be forgot and never brought to mind?
Should auld acquaintance be forgot and auld lang syne?
For auld lang syne, my jo, for auld lang syne,
We'll take a cup o kindness yet, for auld lang syne.

Ayr, High Street 1900 46002

RECIPE

— . —

Broonie

This recipe for gingerbread comes from the Orkney Islands, and calls for fine oatmeal, not the coarse oatmeal used for breakfast porridge. It makes a moist, plain gingerbread with a texture rather like fresh wholemeal bread, which is good eaten slightly warm, spread with butter. Orkney was settled by the Vikings, and the name of Broonie derives from the Norse word 'bruni' for a thick bannock. This recipe calls for buttermilk, which can be bought in most large supermarkets – look for it in the cream section. If buttermilk proves hard to find, use soured milk, either bought or made at home by stirring 1 teaspoonful of lemon juice into 150ml (¼ pint) of milk, then setting it aside for 1 hour to set.

175g/6oz fine oatmeal
175g/6oz plain flour
50g/butter or margarine
2 tablespoonfuls black treacle
1 teaspoonful ground ginger
¾ teaspoonful bicarbonate of soda
1 egg, beaten
150ml/ ¼ pint buttermilk (or soured milk – see above)

Pre-heat the oven to 200°C/400°F/Gas Mark 6.

Sift the flour, ginger and bicarbonate of soda into a bowl. Add the oatmeal and mix well. Rub in the butter or margarine thoroughly, until the mixture resembles coarse breadcrumbs. Heat the treacle in a pan until it is warmed and runny and add it to the mixture, stirring well. Add the well-beaten egg, and then gradually mix in the buttermilk or soured milk. Stir the mixture thoroughly, then turn it into a greased loaf tin and bake in the pre-heated oven for 1-1½ hours, until the gingerbread is well risen and top feels firm to the touch.

— . —

The Oldest Kitchens in Britain?

On the southern shore of the Bay o' Skaill in the Orkney Islands are the remains of the Neolithic village of Skara Brae – one of the most remarkable prehistoric monuments in Europe. The village had been buried under sand for over 40 centuries, but in 1850 a great storm exposed a number of stone buildings that were originally thought to be part of an Iron Age or Pictish village; however, in the 1970s radiocarbon dating showed that the houses were actually far older, dating from the late Neolithic period and inhabited between 3,200BC and 2,200BC. Because the sand had protected the site for so long, the buildings are remarkably well preserved, allowing us a fascinating and intriguing glimpse of life on the Orkneys over 4,000 years ago. The houses all share the same basic design of a large, square room with a central hearth and what appears to be a dresser with shelves, made out of stone, on the wall opposite the doorway – making these rooms probably the oldest kitchens in Britain.

Orkney, Hut 1, Skara Brae 1954 O108026

RECIPE

— . —

Bridescake

A wedding custom from rural Scotland, and particularly the Orkney and Shetland islands, was associated with 'bridescake' (or bride's bonn, or bun), a small shortbread-like cake flavoured with caraway seeds that was cooked on a griddle (called a girdle in Scotland) by the bride's mother on the wedding day. As the bride entered her new home for the first time, her mother would hold the bridescake over her head, and then break it into pieces; if it broke into a number of small pieces, it was taken as a sign that the marriage would be happy, lucky and fruitful. The broken pieces were then given to the unmarried maidens in the wedding party, who would place them under their pillows that night so that they might dream about their future husbands – for this reason it was also known as 'dreaming bread'.

> 150g/5oz self-raising flour
> 50g/2oz butter, softened to room temperature
> 25g/1oz caster sugar
> 25g/1oz caraway seeds
> 3-4 tablespoonfuls milk, to mix

Sift the flour and rub in the butter. Stir in the caster sugar and caraway seeds, and mix it all to a firm dough, adding a little milk as necessary. Roll out the dough to about 1cm (½ inch) thick, and cut it out into a circle about 18cm (7 inch) in diameter (use a plate to cut around). Lightly score the dough with a knife to mark it into 8 segments, but do not cut right through.

Cook the circle of dough on a pre-heated and greased griddle (or girdle) or heavy frying pan over a medium heat for 8-10 minutes, turning it once, until it is golden brown on both sides. Cool on a wire rack.

— . —

A Shetland Woman c1890 A001085

Scotland's Wedding Capital

Gretna Green is the first sizeable town over the English/Scottish border. As a result, the town became popular for runaway marriages of English couples after Lord Hardwicke's act of 1754 abolished irregular marriages in England, but not in Scotland. Once across the bridge, runaways could marry very quickly in accordance with 18th-century Scots law, which required neither banns nor licence. From 1826 the old blacksmith's shop became the most popular place in Gretna for declaratory marriages. After 1856, a residence north of the border of not less than three weeks was required before a marriage could take place. Until 1929, the legal age for marriages in Britain was 12 or above for a girl, and 14 for a boy, although marriages at such a young age were rare. The legal age for marriage was raised to 16 in 1929, although parental consent was required until the age of 18. However, in Scotland no parental consent was required from the age of 16, and this resulted in the continuation of the tradition of young English couples coming to Scotland to marry if they were unable to get their parents' permission. Gretna Green continues to exert a romantic spell, and over 4,000 weddings a year take place in Scotland's 'wedding capital'.

Gretna Green, A Postcard c1940 G163029

RECISE

— . —

Dundee Marmalade Teabread

Dundee is known for 'the three Js' – jute, journalism and jam – but has also been famous for Dundee marmalade since a Mr Keiller acquired a cheap batch of particularly bitter Seville oranges from a Spanish ship that had taken refuge from a storm in Dundee's harbour. Mr Keiller was unable to sell the bitter oranges, so his wife, Mrs Janet Keiller, devised a recipe for marmalade to make use of them, which proved popular. Their son James established the Keiller business, and the company began to produce jam as well as marmalade. This quick and easy recipe uses marmalade to make a delicious teabread. The marmalade helps to keep it moist as well as giving it a lovely flavour. You can use either fine cut or chunky cut marmalade – whichever is your own preference for spreading on your breakfast toast!

> 200g/7oz plain flour
> 1 teaspoonful baking powder
> 1 heaped teaspoonful ground cinnamon
> 115g/4oz butter or margarine, cut into small pieces
> 50g/2oz soft brown sugar
> 4 tablespoonfuls Dundee orange marmalade
> 1 egg, beaten
> 3 tablespoonfuls milk

Pre-heat the oven to 160°C/325°F/Gas Mark 3.

Grease a 1kg (2 lb) loaf tin, and line the base with greased greaseproof paper. Sift the flour, baking powder and cinnamon together into a mixing bowl, add the butter or margarine and rub it in with your fingertips until the mixture resembles fine breadcrumbs, then stir in the sugar. In another bowl, mix together the marmalade, beaten egg and milk, then stir this into the flour and mix thoroughly to make a soft, dropping consistency – add a little more milk if necessary.

Turn the mixture into the prepared loaf tin, and bake in the pre-heated oven for about 1¼ - 1½ hours, until the surface of the cake is firm to the touch. Remove from the oven and leave to cool in the tin for 5 minutes, before turning out onto a wire rack. Peel off the greaseproof paper from the base and leave to cool completely. Serve cut into slices, buttered if liked.

— . —

RECIPE

— . —

Dundee Cake

175g/6oz butter or margarine
175g/6oz soft brown sugar
Half a teaspoonful almond essence
1 teaspoonful ground cinnamon
200g/7oz plain flour
1 level teaspoonful baking powder
175g/6oz sultanas
175g/6oz currants
50g/2oz chopped glacé cherries
25g/1oz ground almonds
3 large eggs, beaten
75g/3oz whole blanched almonds

Pre-heat the oven to 160ºC/325ºF/Gas Mark 3. Grease an 18-20cm (7-8 inch) round cake tin and line the bottom and sides with greased greaseproof paper, allowing the paper to extend about 5cm (2 inches) above the rim of the tin.

Cream together the butter or margarine, sugar, cinnamon and almond essence until it is light and fluffy. Gradually mix the beaten eggs into the creamed mixture, a little at a time, adding a little flour to prevent the mixture curdling. Sift the flour and baking powder into another bowl, then mix in the dried fruit, chopped glacé cherries and ground almonds. Using a large metal spoon, carefully fold in the dried fruit and flour mixture, until it is all evenly blended together. Chop 25g (1oz) of the blanched almonds into very small pieces, and then fold them into the mixture. Turn the mixture into the prepared cake tin, and smooth the surface. Split the remaining blanched almonds lengthways, and use them to decorate the top of the cake, rounded side up, pressing them lightly onto the surface in a pattern of decreasing circles, until it is all covered. Stand the cake tin on a double piece of greaseproof or brown paper on a baking tray. Bake the cake just below the centre of the pre-heated oven for 2½ - 3 hours, until the cake is brown and firm to the touch and a metal skewer inserted into the centre comes out clean. If the cake seems to be browning too quickly, cover the top with a sheet of damp greaseproof paper and reduce the heat to 150ºC/300ºF/Gas Mark 2 for the last hour.

Remove from the oven and allow the cake to cool in the tin for 30 minutes before turning out onto a wire tray to cool completely. Wrap the cake in foil, keeping the lining paper in position, and store in an airtight container. This cake is best left for about one week before eating, to bring out the full flavour, and will keep for several weeks.

— . —

Dundee's Kettle-Bilers

In the 19th and early 20th centuries women played a unique role in the important jute industry of Dundee, which earned the name of 'She-Toon' because so many women were employed within the town's mills and factories. It was often difficult for men to find permanent work in the mills, and many young boys would become unemployed upon completing their apprenticeships because they would then be entitled to adult male rates of pay. The mill owners preferred to employ a female workforce, including married women, as they were paid lower wages than men. The women developed their own sign language in the mills and were able to communicate over the din of the machinery, often to the annoyance of their male supervisors, who did not understand this silent language. With so many women out at work, Dundee's families often experienced a role reversal: the men became 'kettle-bilers' (kettle boilers), so called because they stayed at home to look after the household chores and children.

Dundee, The Alexandra Fountain 1907 D81001

RECIPE

— · —

Abernethy Biscuits

Abernethy Biscuits were not named after the Perthshire town of the same name, but after a certain Dr Abernethy, who devised the recipe.

225g/8oz plain flour
75g/3oz caster sugar
75g/3oz butter or margarine
Half a level teaspoonful baking powder
Half a level teaspoonful caraway seeds
1 tablespoonful milk
1 egg, beaten

Pre-heat the oven to 190°C/375°F/Gas Mark 5.

Sift the flour and baking powder into a mixing bowl then rub in the butter until the mixture resembles fine breadcrumbs. Stir in the sugar and caraway seeds, then add the beaten egg and enough milk to form a stiff dough. Roll out the mixture on a lightly floured surface to about 1cm (½ inch) thick.

Stamp out the dough with a biscuit cutter to make rounds of about 7-8cm (3 inches) in diameter. Prick all over the tops of the biscuits with a fork, then place them onto greased baking trays and bake in the pre-heated oven for about 10 minutes, or until they are golden brown.

Turn out on to a wire tray to cool before eating, and store in an airtight tin.

— · —

RECIPE

~ . ~

Scottish Pancakes

These small pancakes are also known as Drop Scones or Pigs' Ears. They are best eaten whilst still warm, spread with butter, and perhaps Scottish honey or jam, if liked.

115g/4oz plain flour
1 teaspoonful bicarbonate of soda
1 teaspoonful cream of tartar
25g/1oz butter, cut into small pieces
1 egg, beaten
150ml/ ½ pint milk

Lightly grease a griddle (girdle) or a large, heavy-bottomed frying pan, and pre-heat it. Sift the flour, bicarbonate of soda and cream of tartar into a bowl together, then rub in the butter with your fingers until the mixture resembles fine breadcrumbs. Make a well in the centre of the mixture and stir in the beaten egg, together with enough milk to form a thick, creamy batter. Drop spoonfuls of the mixture on to the heated griddle (girdle) or frying pan, spacing them slightly apart.

Cook the pancakes over a steady heat for 2-3 minutes, until bubbles can be seen rising to the surface, then turn them over and cook the other side for a further 2-3 minutes, until the pancakes are golden brown.

Remove the cooked pancakes from the griddle (girdle) or pan and place them inside a folded clean tea towel or napkin on a heated plate to keep warm whilst you cook more pancakes with the remaining mixture – this keeps them soft and moist.

~ . ~

RECIPE

—·—

Scottish Oatcakes

Oatmeal became a staple food in Scotland, because the climate and terrain favoured its growth rather than that of other cereals. Oatcakes can be eaten with cheese, or with jam or marmalade for breakfast, or spread with savoury toppings for snacks or canapés. Some Scottish cooks like to use bacon dripping, saved from the breakfast frying pan, instead of butter or margarine to make their oatcakes. Oatcakes can be made cut into rounds and baked in a moderate oven, but true Scottish oatcakes are made in three-sided triangular shapes, known as 'farls', which have been cooked on a girdle, or griddle.

225g/8oz fine to medium oatmeal
½ teaspoonful of salt
¼ teaspoonful bicarbonate of soda
25g/1oz butter, margarine or bacon fat, melted
About 300ml/ ½ pint hot water

Mix the melted fat with the oatmeal, salt and bicarbonate of soda. Add enough hot water to mix all the ingredients into a soft dough. Turn out the dough onto a surface lightly sprinkled with oatmeal and knead it lightly to remove any cracks in the dough, then roll it out very thinly. Rub the dough with a little more oatmeal then cut it into a very large round, then cut the round into triangular segments, or 'farls'.

Grease a girdle (griddle) or a large, heavy frying pan and pre-heat. Carefully slide the oatcakes onto the pre-heated girdle or pan, and cook over a moderate heat until they begin to curl. They should not be turned over, but, if liked, the second side can be toasted under a hot grill until it is crisp, but not brown.

Oatcakes can be served hot after cooking, or transferred to a wire rack to cool and then stored in an airtight container and eaten cold.

—·—

RECIPE

Ecclefechan Butter Tarts

Ecclefechan is a small town in Dumfries and Galloway, and in 1795 was the birthplace of the influential philosopher and historian Thomas Carlyle. These popular small tarts can be eaten hot or cold.

175g/6oz shortcrust pastry
2 eggs, beaten
175g/6oz soft brown sugar
115g/4oz butter, melted
1 tablespoonful cider apple vinegar (or lemon juice can be used if preferred)
225g/8oz mixed dried fruit – currants, raisins, sultanas
50g/2oz chopped walnuts

Pre-heat the oven to 190°C/375°/Gas Mark 5. Roll out the pastry on a lightly floured surface, and use it to line some greased patty or muffin tins. Mix the sugar, melted butter and beaten eggs together. Stir in the vinegar, then add the mixed fruit and chopped walnuts. Place a spoonful of the mixture into each pastry-lined patty tin. Bake in the pre-heated oven for 20-25 minutes.

Ecclefechan, The Birthplace of Thomas Carlyle E120006

Perth, High Street West 1899 43900

RECIPE

— · —

Inverness Gingernuts

225g/8oz plain flour
2 teaspoonfuls ground ginger
1 teaspoonful ground mixed spice
75g/6oz fine oatmeal
75g/3oz caster sugar
Half a teaspoonful bicarbonate of soda
175g/6oz black treacle
75g/3oz butter, cut into small pieces

Pre-heat the oven to 170°C/325°F/Gas Mark 3.

Put the flour, ginger, mixed spice, oatmeal, sugar and bicarbonate of soda into a large bowl, and mix well together. Melt the treacle and butter in a small saucepan over a moderate heat, then pour it onto the dry ingredients and mix it all together well, to form a smooth dough.

Knead the dough well, then roll it out on a lightly floured surface to about 5mm (¼ inch) thick. Prick all over the surface of the dough with a fork, then use a biscuit cutter to stamp out the dough into small rounds about 6cm (2½ inches) in diameter.

Place the biscuit rounds onto greased baking sheets and bake in the pre-heated oven for 20-25 minutes, until they are firm to the touch. Turn out onto a wire tray to cool completely, then store in an airtight container.

— · —

RECIPE

— . —

Paisley Almond Cakes

These little cakes are light and fluffy on the inside, and have a delicious crunchy exterior when they are freshly made. This amount makes about 12 cakes.

50g/2oz cornflour
50g/2oz ground rice
1 teaspoonful baking powder
75g/3oz butter
75g/3oz caster sugar
40g/1½ oz ground almonds
2 eggs, beaten

Pre-heat the oven to 180°C/350°F/Gas Mark 4. Grease 12 patty tins, and line them with paper cases if you wish.

Sieve the cornflour, ground rice and baking powder together into a bowl. In a separate bowl, or in a food mixer, cream the butter and sugar together until it is light and fluffy. Gradually beat in the eggs and the cornflour mixture, alternating between them. When the mixture is white and creamy, lightly stir in the ground almonds.

Half fill the patty tins with the mixture, then bake in the pre-heated oven for 10-15 minutes, until they are risen and golden brown, and firm to the touch. Remove from the oven and leave to cool in the tins for 5 minutes, before turning out on a wire rack to cool completely.

— . —

RECITE

— . —

Scottish Morning Rolls

These soft bread rolls are also known as Scottish Baps, and are best eaten warm from the oven, soon after baking. They are often served for breakfast in Scotland, perhaps with a fried egg and bacon, which is why they are known as Morning Rolls. If preferred, the dough can be made the night before, and left overnight in a bowl inside a greased polythene bag in the fridge for its 'first rising'. In the morning, take the dough out of the fridge and leave it for about 30 minutes to reach room temperature, then turn it onto a floured surface for its second kneading, and follow the recipe from there.

> 450g/1 lb strong white unbleached flour, and a little extra for dusting the rolls after baking
> 2 level teaspoonfuls of salt
> 150ml/ ¼ pint lukewarm water
> 150ml/ ¼ pint lukewarm milk
> 1 level teaspoonful of sugar
> 25g/1oz fresh yeast, or 15g/ ½ oz dried yeast
> 25g/1oz melted fat – butter, margarine or lard

Mix the yeast with warm water and the sugar, and leave in a warm place to activate until it is frothy – about 10-15 minutes. Mix the flour and salt together in a warmed bowl, and make a well in the centre. Pour in the activated yeast mixture, together with the warmed milk and the melted fat, and mix it all well together. Cover the bowl with a tea towel, and leave the mixture to 'rest' for a few minutes, then flour your hands and turn out the dough onto a lightly floured surface and knead it until it is soft, smooth and puffy. Place the dough in the bowl, cover with a damp cloth and place the bowl in a polythene bag. Leave it in a warm place for about one hour, until the dough has risen and has doubled in size.

Pre-heat the oven to 200°C/400°F/Gas Mark 6, and grease and lightly flour two baking sheets. Turn out the dough onto a floured surface, knock back and knead again. Cut the dough into 10-12 small pieces, form them into balls and use a rolling pin to gently shape and flatten them into round rolls. Put the rolls on to the prepared baking sheets, spacing them well apart, and lightly dust with flour. Cover the trays with a cloth and leave in warm place for about 30 minutes, to allow the rolls to rise. Use your three middle fingers to press onto the middle of each roll with your finger (this helps to prevent the rolls 'blistering'), then place the trays in the pre-heated oven and bake the rolls for about 15-20 minutes until lightly browned but not crispy. Dust with a little more flour, and allow the rolls to cool slightly on a wire rack before serving whilst they are still warm.

— . —

Loch Acray, The Trossachs Church 1871 L89001

INDEX OF PHOTOGRAPHS

INDEX OF RECIPES

—·—

—·—

FRITH PRODUCTS & SERVICES

Francis Frith would doubtless be pleased to know that the pioneering publishing venture he started in 1860 still continues today. Over a hundred and forty years later, The Francis Frith Collection continues in the same innovative tradition and is now one of the foremost publishers of vintage photographs in the world. Some of the current activities include:

INTERIOR DECORATION

Today Frith's photographs can be seen framed and as giant wall murals in thousands of pubs, restaurants, hotels, banks, retail stores and other public buildings throughout the country. In every case they enhance the unique local atmosphere of the places they depict and provide reminders of gentler days in an increasingly busy and frenetic world.

PRODUCT PROMOTIONS

Frith products are used by many major companies to promote the sales of their own products or to reinforce their own history and heritage. Frith promotions have been used by Hovis bread, Courage beers, Scots Porage Oats, Colman's mustard, Cadbury's foods, Mellow Birds coffee, Dunhill pipe tobacco, Guinness, and Bulmer's Cider.

GENEALOGY AND FAMILY HISTORY

As the interest in family history and roots grows world-wide, more and more people are turning to Frith's photographs of Great Britain for images of the towns, villages and streets where their ancestors lived; and, of course, photographs of the churches and chapels where their ancestors were christened, married and buried are an essential part of every genealogy tree and family album.

FRITH PRODUCTS

All Frith photographs are available Framed or just as Mounted Prints and Posters (size 23 x 16 inches). These may be ordered from the address below. Other products available are - Address Books, Calendars, Jigsaws, Canvas Prints, Postcards and local and prestige books.

THE INTERNET

Already 120,000 Frith photographs can be viewed and purchased on the internet through the Frith websites and a myriad of partner sites.

For more detailed information on Frith products, look at this site:
www.francisfrith.com

See the complete list of Frith Books at: www.francisfrith.com

This web site is regularly updated with the latest list of publications from The Francis Frith Collection. If you wish to buy books relating to another part of the country that your local bookshop does not stock, you may purchase on-line.

For further information, trade, or author enquiries please contact us at the address below:

The Francis Frith Collection, 6 Oakley Business Park, Wylye Road, Dinton, Wiltshire SP3 5EU.

Tel: +44 (0)1722 716 376 Fax: +44 (0)1722 716 881 Email: sales@francisfrith.co.uk

---

See Frith products on the internet at **www.francisfrith.com**

FREE PRINT OF YOUR CHOICE

+ £2.63 POSTAGE

Mounted Print
Overall size 14 x 11 inches (355 x 280mm)

Choose any Frith photograph in this book.
Simply complete the Voucher opposite and return it with your remittance for £2.63 (to cover postage) and we will print the photograph of your choice in SEPIA (size 11 x 8 inches) and supply it in a cream mount with a burgundy rule line (overall size 14 x 11 inches).
Please note: aerial photographs and photographs with a reference number starting with a "Z" are not Frith photographs and cannot be supplied under this offer. Offer valid for delivery to one UK address only.

PLUS: **Order additional Mounted Prints at HALF PRICE - £10.00 each** (normally £20.00)
If you would like to order more Frith prints from this book, possibly as gifts for friends and family, you can buy them at half price (with no additional postage costs).

PLUS: **Have your Mounted Prints framed**
For an extra £19.50 per print you can have your mounted print(s) framed in an elegant polished wood and gilt moulding, overall size 16 x 13 inches (no additional postage required).

IMPORTANT!
These special prices are only available if you use this form to order. You must use the ORIGINAL VOUCHER on this page (no copies permitted). We can only despatch to one UK address. This offer cannot be combined with any other offer.

For Further information about local books, please contact: localbooks@uberdistribution.co.uk

As a customer your name & address will be stored by Frith but not sold or rented to third parties. Your data will be used for the purpose of this promotion only.

Send completed Voucher form to:
**The Francis Frith Collection,
6 Oakley Business Park, Wylye Road,
Dinton, Wiltshire SP3 5EU**

CHOOSE A PHOTOGRAPH FROM THIS BOOK

Voucher for **FREE** and *Reduced Price Frith Prints*

Please do not photocopy this voucher. Only the original is valid, so please fill it in, cut it out and return it to us with your order.

Picture ref no	Page no	Qty	Mounted @ £10.00	Framed + £19.00	Total Cost £
		1	Free of charge*	£	£
			£10.00	£	£
			£10.00	£	£
			£10.00	£	£
			£10.00	£	£
			£10.00	£	£

Please allow 28 days for delivery.
Offer available to one UK address only

* Postage £2.63

Total Order Cost £

Title of this book . . . .

I enclose a cheque/postal order for £ . . . .
made payable to 'The Francis Frith Collection'

OR please debit my Mastercard / Visa / Maestro card, details below

Card Number:

Issue No (Maestro only):   Valid from (Maestro):

Card Security Number: Expires:

Signature:

Name Mr/Mrs/Ms . . . .

Address . . . .

. . . .

. . . .

. . . . Postcode . . . .

Daytime Tel No . . . .

Email . . . .

Free Print – see overleaf

Can you help us with information about any of the Frith photographs in this book?

We are gradually compiling an historical record for each of the photographs in the Frith archive. It is always fascinating to find out the names of the people shown in the pictures, as well as insights into the shops, buildings and other features depicted.

If you recognize anyone in the photographs in this book, or if you have information not already included in the author's caption, do let us know. We would love to hear from you, and will try to publish it in future books or articles.

An Invitation from The Francis Frith Collection to Share Your Memories

The 'Share Your Memories' feature of our website allows members of the public to add personal memories relating to the places featured in our photographs, or comment on others already added. Seeing a place from your past can rekindle forgotten or long held memories. Why not visit the website, find photographs of places you know well and add YOUR story for others to read and enjoy? We would love to hear from you!

www.francisfrith.com/memories

Our production team

Frith books are produced by a small dedicated team at offices near Salisbury. Most have worked with the Frith Collection for many years. All have in common one quality: they have a passion for the Frith Collection.

Frith Books and Gifts

We have a wide range of books and gifts available on our website utilising our photographic archive, many of which can be individually personalised.

www.francisfrith.com